Language Change

'This book provides a readable, entertaining and informative introduction to issues in language change. The examples and exercises require little metalinguistic knowledge, introducing linguistic concepts and terminology gradually. The texts and exercises are well-chosen and will stimulate discussion.'

Joan Beal, *University of Sheffield*, UK.

'An excellent resource for A Level Language. It opens up the field, going beyond narrow definitions of language change and offering lively textual examples and commentaries to support students' learning.'

Barbara Bleiman, Advisory Teacher at *The English and Media Centre*, UK.

The INTERTEXT series has been specifically designed to meet the needs of contemporary English Language Studies. *Working with Texts: A core introduction to language analysis* (second edition, 2001) is the foundation text, which is complemented by a range of 'satellite' titles. These provide students with hands-on practical experience of textual analysis through special topics, and can be used individually or in conjunction with *Working with Texts*.

Language Change:

◎ examines the way external factors have influenced and are influencing language change
◎ focuses on how changing social contexts are reflected in language use
◎ looks at how language change operates within different genres, such as problem pages, sports reports and recipes
◎ provides lively examples from interperson   including letters, emails, postcards and text messages
◎ considers attitudes towards language cha
◎ includes a unit which describes various f
◎ features a full index of terms.

Adrian Beard teaches at the University of Newcastle upo   author, series editor of the Routledge A Level English Guides and the Inte   es, and is Chief Examiner for English at A Level.

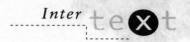

The Intertext series

The Routledge INTERTEXT series aims to develop readers' understanding of how texts work. It does this by showing some of the designs and patterns in the language from which they are made, by placing texts within the contexts in which they occur, and by exploring relationships between them.

The series consists of a foundation text, *Working with Texts: A core introduction to language analysis*, which looks at language aspects essential for the analysis of texts, and a range of satellite texts. These apply aspects of language to a particular topic area in more detail. They complement the core text and can also be used alone, providing the user has the foundation skills furnished by the core text.

Benefits of using this series:

- **Multi-disciplinary** – provides a foundation for the analysis of texts, supporting students who want to achieve a detailed focus on language.

- **Accessible** – no previous knowledge of language analysis is assumed, just an interest in language use.

- **Student-friendly** – contains activities relating to texts studied, commentaries after activities, highlighted key terms, suggestions for further reading and an index of terms.

- **Interactive** – offers a range of task-based activities for both class use and self-study.

- **Tried and tested** – written by a team of respected teachers and practitioners whose ideas and activities have been trialled independently.

The series editors:

Adrian Beard was until recently Head of English at Gosforth High School, and now works at the University of Newcastle upon Tyne. He is a Chief Examiner for AS and A Level English Literature. He has written and lectured extensively on the subjects of literature and language. His publications include *Texts and Contexts* (Routledge).

Angela Goddard is Head of Programme for Language and Human Communication at the University College of York St John, and is Chair of Examiners for A Level English Language. Her publications include *Researching Language* (second edition, 2000).

Core textbook:
Working with Texts: A core introduction to language analysis
(second edition, 2001)
Ronald Carter, Angela Goddard, Danuta Reah, Keith Sanger and
Maggie Bowring

Satellite titles:

Language and Gender
Angela Goddard and Lindsey Meân Patterson

The Language of Advertising: Written texts
(second edition, 2002)
Angela Goddard

The Language of Children
Julia Gillen

The Language of Comics
Mario Saraceni

The Language of Conversation
Francesca Pridham

The Language of Drama
Keith Sanger

The Language of Fiction
Keith Sanger

The Language of Humour
Alison Ross

The Language of ICT: Information and communication technology
Tim Shortis

The Language of Magazines
Linda McLoughlin

The Language of Newspapers
(second edition, 2002)
Danuta Reah

The Language of Poetry
John McRae

The Language of Politics
Adrian Beard

The Language of Speech and Writing
Sandra Cornbleet and
Ronald Carter

The Language of Sport
Adrian Beard

The Language of Television
Jill Marshall and Angela Werndly

The Language of Websites
Mark Boardman

The Language of Work
Almut Koester

Language
Change

© Adrian Beard

Routledge
Taylor & Francis Group

LONDON AND NEW YORK

First published 2004
by Routledge
11 New Fetter Lane, London EC4P 4EE

Simultaneously published in the USA and Canada
by Routledge
29 West 35th Street, New York, NY 10001

Routledge is an imprint of the Taylor & Francis Group

Typeset in Stone Sans/Stone Serif by
Florence Production Ltd, Stoodleigh, Devon
Printed and bound in Great Britain by
TJ International Ltd, Padstow, Cornwall

British Library Cataloguing in Publication Data
A catalogue record for this book is available from the
British Library

Library of Congress Cataloging in Publication Data
A catalog record for this book has been requested

ISBN 0–415–32055–0 (hbk)
ISBN 0–415–32056–9 (pbk)

contents

Acknowledgements ix

Unit one: Context and language change   1

Internal/external   1
Ideology in texts   6
Assumed reading positions   9
Summary   14

Unit two: Genre and change   15

Generic conventions   15
Social functions/language structures   18
Problem pages   18
Sports writing   22
What's for pudding?   28
Summary   33

Unit three: Interpersonal communication genres
       and change   35

Writing home   35
Formality and informality   39
Telephone voices   43
Multimodal communication   44
Emails   45
Text messages   49
Chat-groups   51
Summary   54

Unit four: Visual representation and change   55

Semiotics and representation   55
Graphemic symbols   56
Finding meanings in visual representation   57

Visual sophistication   60
Visual representation in multimodal texts   61
Production/reception   63
Verbal/visual   64
Summary   70

Unit five: Attitudes to language change   **71**

Public debate   71
Taboo   73
Change or difference?   74
Prescription/description   77
Plain English   79
Political correctness   82
Self-labels   86
Summary   88

Unit six: Internal aspects of change   **89**

Lexical change   90
Spelling   91
Punctuation   93
Grammar   93
Meaning and etymology   94
Pronunciation   95

Answers and commentaries   99
References   109
Index of terms   111

acknowledgements

With particular thanks to Angela Goddard for her help throughout the writing of this book.

Bank of Scotland Investment Service, recruitment advertisement reproduced with the permission of the Bank of Scotland Investment Service.

Thanks to Jennifer Kirk, Rosie Wayman, Becca Wood and Andrew Turner, students on BA (Hons) Human Communication at Manchester Metropolitan University, 1999–2002 for their chat-room log.

Leeds & Holbeck, credit card advertisement reproduced with the permission of Leeds & Holbeck Building Society and Morgan Stanley Dean Witter Credit Card Services Limited.

The Portman Group, 'Don't Do Drunk' postcard reproduced with the permission of The Portman Group.

Gary Rhodes, extract from *New British Classics* reproduced with the permission of BBC Worldwide Limited. Copyright © Gary Rhodes 1999.

William Shakespeare, Bodleian Library, University of Oxford for Dedication from William Shakespeare's *Venus and Adonis* 1593. Reference (shelfmark) Arch.G e.31 (2).

Hilary Spurling, 'The Lord of Devonshire His Pudding', recipe from *Elinor Fettiplace's Receipt Book: Elizabethan country house* reproduced with the permission of Penguin.

The Science & Society Picture Library, Italy/Cornwall Great Western Railway (GWR) poster, reproduced with permission of The Science & Society Picture Library.

Bill Leckie, the *Scottish Sun* match report, reproduced with permission of the *Scottish Sun*.

Context and language change

Broadly speaking it is possible to explore ideas about language change by looking at what Suzanne Romaine (1998) calls the *internal* history of a language and the *external* history of a language. Traditionally the topic of language change has tended to be approached via the internal route, looking at the way new words have been formed, the influence of dictionaries on spellings and meanings and so forth. This process is described as internal because it looks at what has happened in a language without referring to any other outside factors.

Throughout this book there will be reference to some of these internal issues, and they will be summarised in the final unit, but the general approach will be to look at the way *external* factors have influenced and are influencing language change. This unit looks in particular at the way changing social contexts are reflected in language. In order to show that language change is an ongoing process, rather than just an historical study, all of the data in this unit will have been produced in the twentieth and twenty-first centuries.

Activity

Look at Text 1: A Career in the Bank which was a recruitment advertisement in a grammar school magazine in 1967. The magazine was an official school publication; although much of it was written by students, it was vetted by staff and sent to parents. The advertisement was written by the bank and placed on the back cover of the magazine.

Prepare some notes for a commentary on this text, using the following framework to help you. Look first at what have been called 'internal aspects', some of the technical features of the language used, and then broaden your analysis to look at the 'external aspects' listed below.

Internal aspects

◎   What vocabulary is used in the text and how does it relate to current usage?

◎   What spellings are used in the text and how do they relate to current usage?

◎   What meanings are found in the text and how do they relate to current usage?

◎   How is grammar used in the text and how does it relate to current usage?

External aspects

◎   Who is writing the text?

◎   For what purpose are they writing the text?

◎   For what audience are they writing the text?

◎   What is the text's level of formality?

◎   What attitudes, values and assumptions are in the text?

◎   What kind of text are they producing?

All of the above form part of the *context* of the text.

(This is an edited version of *A Framework for Looking at Texts*, published by LINC in *Language in the National Curriculum*, p. 84.)

A CAREER
IN
THE BANK

Never before have opportunities for young people been as promising as they are today in _____ bank. Here is a brief outline of the career that awaits you there.

For ambitious young men

The bank wants young men of character and integrity, with a good standard of general education. Given these qualifications and an aptitude for the job, there is no reason why you should not find yourself a branch manager in your thirties, with a salary upwards of £1865 and the chance of doubling your pay by the time you are 50. Looking ahead, you could be one of those managers whose salary exceeds £5000 a year – a man with a big job, full of interest and responsibility. A goal worth striving for!

And there's scope for girls as well

The women's salary scale runs from £340 on entry to a minimum of £735 at 31. A wide range of positions apart from the usual secretarial and bookkeeping duties are now open to women in the bank. For instance girls can – and do – become cashiers, supervisors, income tax specialists and officers in the Executor and Trustee department. We even have two women branch managers. If you are keen to get on, prepared to study and not afraid of work, why not think about banking as *your* career. Incidentally, a girl who marries after five years' service in the bank qualifies for a gratuity.

Commentary

An internal approach to studying language change looks at such areas as vocabulary, spelling, meanings of words, grammar and compares usage in 'old' texts with usage found today. In this text, very little is different from what we would find today. But if you look at the external aspects of this text, viewing it more as a social document, it seems to belong to a different age. You simply would not find anything like this nowadays.

If we look first at some of the internal aspects of the text, we find that on a lexical level there are no words here which will cause modern readers any real problems in terms of *spelling* or *meaning*. It could well be that in the modern world of banking branch managers are no longer in evidence, and bookkeeping will have been replaced by computers. The idea of book-keeping may puzzle younger readers who are brought up in a world of different technology and computers and who do not remember the laborious longhand methods of bookkeeping that were once commonplace. Even though this is an advertisement for a job, which might lead you to expect some specialist vocabulary, there is not a great deal here.

The idea of being a 'man with a big job' may also seem odd, even amusing, given some possible interpretations of the phrase today. There has been a slight *semantic* shift. The bald use of 'big' makes it seem rather unspecific.

In terms of *syntax* and *grammar*, there are some differences from what we might expect today in an advertisement addressed to a young audience. The syntax is quite complex, for example. Take the sentence:

> 'Looking ahead, you could be one of those managers whose salary exceeds £5000 a year – a man with a big job, full of interest and responsibility.'

It begins with a **subordinate clause** 'looking ahead'; followed by a **modal verb** 'could'; a **relative clause** beginning with 'whose'; a dash signifying more to come; and two **noun phrases** at the end, 'a man with a big job' and '(a job) full of interest and responsibility'. Even if you are not sure how to label the parts of the sentence, it will be clear that this is more complex than you might expect to find nowadays, where the syntax would probably be less cluttered, the message more direct.

This complex syntax and sophisticated grammar mean that the text inevitably seems quite formal to modern readers. Although the constructed ideal reader of the text, or **narratee**, is sometimes addressed as 'you', and in one case 'your' is highlighted by italics, it is not done consistently. The first section begins with the much less personal 'young men' for example. The

4

reference to specific sums of money (sometimes as 'salary' sometimes as 'pay') also gives a sense of being very precise. It could be argued, incidentally, that although apparently addressed to 'young men' and 'girls too', the real audience here is their parents who would have been deciding key aspects of their children's future in a way which is not so much the case nowadays.

In terms of appearance and design, its **graphology**, this text is dull and uninteresting – certainly a modern bank advertisement today would be likely to play with different fonts, angles of type etc. A modern advertisement would also probably have **semantic** play in a way that this one does not. We expect advertisements these days to be clever, to do something creative with words and meanings. Here, though, what you see is what you get. Although there is a headline and two further sub-headlines, they signal what is to come without expecting the reader to do any real work.

Overall then this text has some features which are quite formal, and one or two which suggest that the authors are aware that the audience is specifically young (it is in a school magazine) without going very far in appealing directly to them. But for all that, judged against the internal technical criteria which are used to discuss language change, this text does not seem very unusual:

◎   it uses vocabulary that is easily recognised;

◎   the spelling is as we expect today;

◎   the meanings of words are very little different from today;

◎   it is grammatically quite complex but not difficult to understand.

Yet, of course, it would be ludicrous to suggest that this text is anything other than very dated, belonging to a different time and a completely different set of social values.

This can be explored by first asking what kind of text is this? What is its **genre**? It is not enough to say that it is an advertisement – the context of the advertisement needs to be explored. It is a written text, placed in a school magazine, but a sort of magazine that no longer exists in most schools or colleges. It was appealing to grammar school students, who by the fact that they went to grammar school would have a 'good standard of education'. It was placed by a bank seeking to recruit workers in a commercial sphere which employed lots of people to do routine jobs.

It is, then, the **attitudes and values** of the authors and the audience which show a real difference from those held today. One reason why this text seems so outdated concerns the assumptions it makes about institutional working practices. It is highly unlikely these days that a school or college magazine would include advertisements for jobs – for higher education courses maybe, but not for jobs. And even more unusual than this is the assumption that once you start working for a bank, you will stay there for life – unless of course you are a woman who gets married. It is highly unlikely that employers would suggest such life service in the twenty-first century, or that prospective workers would find the idea attractive if they did.

The second and most obvious reason why this advertisement strikes modern readers as so unusual lies in its attitude to gender. It reflects assumptions about the roles of men and women which not only no longer apply, but which are not allowed to apply. Equal opportunities legislation means that it should no longer be possible to pay men more than women, or to suggest that some jobs are more suited to men and some to women.

How does the text show these outdated attitudes, apart from different jobs and pay rates? It sees 'young men' as 'ambitious', and the word 'men' is the only one used to signify being male. When it comes to females, though, they are referred to as 'girls' as well as 'women', without any apparent logical difference between the two. So it is 'a girl who marries' rather than a 'woman', for example. There is also no reference to married men, because their working conditions are not affected by their marital status.

The reference to 'a girl who marries after five years' service in the bank qualifies for a gratuity' is actually quite hard to understand nowadays, although in 1967 it presumably carried more obvious significance. It appears to mean that the bank wants women to wait before they marry, because it assumes that women marry as soon as they can, and that they then leave work to become housewives and/or mothers.

IDEOLOGY IN TEXTS

This first text, then, has indicated some of the linguistic areas which can be looked at under the heading of 'language change', such as spelling, vocabulary, meaning, grammar, but has also highlighted the fact that language change is bound up with social change. In other words we have explored the **ideology** which lies behind this text, especially the ways in which it sees men and women, and compared it to the dominant ideology which exists in our culture and in our time.

After exploring its highly specific context we need to be careful though – we cannot simply turn to the date of this text, 1967, and make generalised claims for language use at that time. One example of a particular genre of writing does not in itself prove a general rule. Nor can we assume that nobody at the time saw in the text what we see now – it is always possible to resist a dominant ideology.

So far we have seen that awareness of a text's genre, its context in terms of the time and place of its production and the attitudes it expresses to its expected readership have all been significant in evaluating a text from a perspective of language change. This unit will continue to explore some of these issues by looking at two further texts which belong to specific genres.

Activity

Text 2: The Kid-Glove Collier is taken from a story of the same name which first appeared in a book of stories called *Monster Book for Boys*. Although there is no publication date, it would appear that the book was published in 1947. None of the stories in the book have named authors. To understand this extract, one piece of contextual information you need to know involves what were called Bevin boys. Named after the politician Ernest Bevin, these were young men who instead of being conscripted into the forces during the Second World War were selected by lottery to work in the mines and so help the war effort. It is generally recognised now that this was often a very traumatic experience for young men from non-mining communities, who were faced with a different culture and often shocking working conditions.

Bearing in mind the genre of this text – it is a sort of pulp fiction 'for boys' – and using the framework used earlier on p. 2 write a commentary on this text from a perspective of language change. In doing this you could look at:

◎ how the character of Bob is presented in the story;

◎ how mining and miners are represented;

◎ how masculinity in general is represented;

◎ the likely audience for this story;

◎ 'internal' aspects of language use such as vocabulary and grammar;

◎ the possible purposes that can be seen behind the attitudes and values found in this text.

In addition you could consider how this story might continue.

(Note: there is a commentary on this activity on p. 99.)

Text 2: The Kid-Glove Collier

The following extract forms the start of a story published in *Monster Book for Boys* (1947).

BOB MORTON sent the point of his pick eating into the blackness of the coal face with a rhythmic movement of his wrists.

by BEN DRAPER

He was lying on his side in the narrow gallery, his miner's lamp perched upon a ledge forward of his head so that it threw its warm light upon the seam of coal he was attacking.

It was warm work, yet Bob liked it.

When his architectural studies had been interrupted and, as a Bevin boy, he had been sent down the pit, he thought he would detest the work. However, he had soon found there was something worthwhile about this wresting of black diamonds from the earth. It was a man's job and Bob found only one fault with it.

Not the darkness, or the dirt, or the trickling damp of the pit. Those didn't trouble him, for he was young, strong and healthy for his seventeen years, and hard work, danger and darkness didn't worry him.

What did worry him was the resentment of the other pit lads. Because he spoke a little better, because he brought his food wrapped in a clean table napkin, because of little things like that, they thought him a snob. Most of all they were contemptuous of his gloves.

Drawing was a passion with Bob and because he disliked getting his hands mauled with dirt, broken with the jagged rocks, so that he couldn't use a drawing-board, he wore gloves.

He had stood a lot of twitting on account of them. Even the older colliers with rough good-nature had smiled about Bob's gloves.

"The Kid-Glove Collier," they had named him.

> Bob could stand that, but Dick Haslam's name for him made Bob's face prickle with hot rage.
>
> "The Pansy Pitboy!" Dick Haslam had dubbed him, though not in Bob's hearing. Dick was a lad of Bob's own age, who resented more than the others that Bob had come down the pit. Bob had tackled him about it once.
>
> "What have you against me, Haslam?" he asked.
>
> "You thinking you can come down here and learn in five minutes what it's taken some of us years to learn," Dick had answered. "Besides, the pit's no place for softies, with gloves and things!"

ASSUMED READING POSITIONS

The next text to be explored in this unit is taken from an American book *What a Young Wife Ought to Know* by Mrs Emma F. Angell Drake and published in 1901. It was part of a series called *Pure Books on Avoided Subjects* which also had a companion volume entitled *What a Young Husband Ought to Know*. Each chapter starts with a résumé of what is to follow, which is given here. The text which follows is an edited extract from Chapter V.

Activity

One way of categorising this text in terms of its genre is to say that it is an advisory text. This book is a forerunner of the advice columns which still appear in many magazines and newspapers, often in an 'agony aunt' format.

Read Text 3: What a Young Wife Ought to Know and then complete the questions below.

◎ What techniques of persuasion are used in this extract?

◎ What assumptions are made about women's behaviour?

◎ How are men 'positioned' in this text – in other words what assumptions are made about male behaviour?

◎ When you have answered the three questions above, summarise the attitudes and values which lie behind this text.

Text 3: What a Young Wife Ought to Know

CHAPTER V.

WHAT SHALL A YOUNG WIFE EXPECT TO BE TO HER HUSBAND?

The Young Wife Should Seek to be Her Husband's Equal, but not His Counterpart.—The Recognized Centre of the Home.—Woman's True Greatness.—Man's Helpmeet.—Mrs. Gladstone's Part in Her Husband's Greatness.—Should Attract Her Husband from the Club to the Home.—Continuing to be Attractive in Dress and Manners.—Should Accept both Wifehood and Motherhood.—Should Keep Pace with His Mental Growth.—Guarding Against Improper Use of Literary Clubs, Reading Circles, etc.—Solomon's Picture of the Model Young Wife.—A Converted Heathen's Estimate of His Christian Wife . . 65–72

Every young wife should be a good home-maker. An Eastern proverb says: "The wife is the household." And the Japanese say, "The house rests upon the mother." O woman! guard your treasure sacredly, this most priceless marriage gift, the title and blessing of home-keeper. You should make the home so attractive that no club can win the husband away from it in his leisure hours. You should make it, not only a haven of rest for him, but a place for delightful entertainments of his friends at all suitable times. However, the thoughtful husband will not invite his friends to his home, as a rule, without a word sent to his wife, that she may make any little needed preparation, and so be her happiest self with the guests.

The young wife should take not less, but more pains to make herself as attractive after as before marriage. A soiled ribbon, an untidy toilet, may seem trifling things, but they tell much of the esteem in which she holds her husband and her home. Not less but more care is needed to retain the love and respect of the man of her choice, than to win it. The pretty dress, the color of the ribbon, the manner of dressing the hair, are not affected, but chosen deliberately because she knows they are pleasing to him.

She should be the willing mother of his children. Marriage comprehends not only wifehood, but motherhood. To-day this is hardly believed by the many, and we may well mourn it as fatal, not only to the future of the American race, but to the best and highest interests of the home.

She should seek to keep pace with him in his mental growth, and never for a moment think that she is advancing his highest interests when she is denying herself that which would contribute to her development in order that he may advance. The marriage contract is not so one-sided a matter as this.

The thoughtful husband will never allow such self-abnegation on the part of the wife. What he reads, she should read; and if she have not the time, he should read it aloud, while her hands are busy with the household cares.

Commentary

The **rhetorical** or persuasive techniques in this text are based upon the modal verbs 'ought' (in the title of the book) 'should' (when referring to the wife) and 'will' (when referring to the husband). Both 'ought' and 'should' in contemporary usage can suggest either duty and certainty (as in 'he ought to know better') or desirability and probability (as in 'ten minutes should be long enough'). In this text, women's behaviour follows the pattern of 'every wife/should', as can be seen in the opening line. Clearly this use of the word 'should' is used in the sense of duty and necessity, rather than the less forceful sense of desirability. The fact that 'will' is used for men, though, does give a subtle difference. Men's behaviour is more of a given fixed point – women's behaviour needs to be encouraged by clear-cut advice about duty.

In a similar way to the bank advertisement seen earlier, women are labelled and addressed in a number of ways. The text sometimes talks about all young wives, sometimes addresses an individual narratee as 'you', and also invokes 'woman' meaning all women. A proverb and another culture are used to support the arguments, and there is also the invocation/instruction – 'O woman! Guard your treasure'. There is no possibility here that women lead anything other than identical lives – there are no exceptions to the rules laid down.

Expectations of women's behaviour can be seen in the frequent references to house and home. A wife is a homemaker, a 'home-keeper' and a mother. She must also keep herself attractive and be intelligent, although her intelligence should be modelled on her husband's. She must work hard to keep her man, making sure that she dresses up to please him rather than herself. Note, though, that motherhood is being questioned in the world outside this text; in a rare moment of doubt this text warns of dire consequences if motherhood is doubted.

Men's behaviour is also governed by expectations, sometimes mentioned explicitly, sometimes more implicitly. Men have a life outside the home, presumably work, and they have 'leisure hours'. They can be thoughtful, not impulsive, pleased by outward attractiveness, intellectual in their interests. By implication they have physical needs which the wife must satisfy – 'She should be the willing mother of his children' is a sentence packed with meanings. There is a sense though that not all men are 'thoughtful'. A good wife will modify a man's behaviour, to make sure he does not stray and go to the 'club'.

Overall the text has many values and assumptions which lie behind the advice. This is a middle-class world where money does not need to be mentioned, where a home is taken for granted, where a pretty dress is easily available. As with 'The Kid-Glove Collier' earlier, it is worth remembering that readers did not necessarily live in such a world, but it was a world they could aspire to. It was attractive because it presented a world where both women and men are locked into rules of behaviour that are clearly defined.

Because this text is about marriage, women's duty etc., and because we know it is an 'old' text, we may readily jump to the conclusion that its only relevance is as a quaint piece of social history. However, if you look at examples of the way women and men are represented in many contemporary texts, such as teenage magazines for girls, men's lifestyle magazines etc., you may well find that many of the same attitudes and values are still being put forward, albeit in a rather different format.

Extension

1   Language change, even over a small period of time, can often best be highlighted by comparing texts which are similar in purpose and audience. This can be done by comparing the bank advertisement earlier in this unit with another advertisement for bank recruitment, this time from a national newspaper in 2003.

Text 4: Bank of Scotland Investment Service Recruitment

Year 1 OTE £40k - £45k + car + benefits
UK-wide opportunities

Financial Sales

'It's time for a change'

Companies that prosper need to remember that they have no right to the loyalty of customers - they must earn it through the best strategies, products and service, delivered by outstanding people.

HBOS plc is a positive force for change in the financial services industry, with a clear strategy and a market leading position in long-term savings and investment. **Bank of Scotland Investment Service (BoSIS)** is key to that strategy, providing our high net worth client base - comprising companies, partnerships, company directors, senior managers and self-employed professionals - with comprehensive, bespoke financial planning services through our Private and Business Client Divisions. *We need more outstanding people.*

You're good at what you do. You have a successful track record in a profession, business or top-end sales environment. You know the value of good preparation, individual initiative and hard work. You're ambitious. You want a challenging career. You want to build professional relationships and deliver high quality, client focused products and service. You want the opportunity to gain the rewards that reflect your efforts and achievements. *Here is that opportunity.*

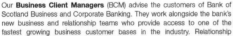

Our **Business Client Managers** (BCM) advise the customers of Bank of Scotland Business and Corporate Banking. They work alongside the bank's new business and relationship teams who provide access to one of the fastest growing business customer bases in the industry. Relationship management is a key part of the role, with a need to go the extra mile in terms of advice and customer service to both clients and colleagues. Financial Services experience in the business/corporate market is essential and the potential rewards substantial.

Our **Private Client Managers** (PCM), based at one of our 26 branches across the UK, are responsible for identifying high quality new business opportunities from existing clients, referrals and by direct approach. Referral sources include the Bank of Scotland Private Banking arm and leads from highly targeted business campaigns. A key task of the PCM is to analyse and understand our clients' financial situation and identify effective solutions to meet their changing needs. Our PCMs come from a wide range of professional and business backgrounds, not necessarily with direct financial services experience.

To be successful you must possess excellent commercial, sales and communications skills and be comfortable dealing with senior business people, as equals. Resourceful, resilient and resolute, you will need the ability to understand complex legislation and products. You will receive the very best training and first class sales support to enable you to build on your success to date.

We offer a competitive remuneration package with open-ended performance bonus and generous share schemes. Established sales professionals will usually earn over £60,000 with our top people achieving even more. Benefits also include car, BUPA, concessionary mortgage and 26 days holiday.

Time for a change? **Then please ring 01296 386066 for an information pack, or visit www.bosinvestment.co.uk where you can download a Personal History Form (application form) and information booklet. Last date for receipt of completed application forms is 30 May 2003.**

*Equal opportunities for all -
our policy is as simple as that.*

BANK OF SCOTLAND
INVESTMENT SERVICE

2   This unit began with Text 1: A Career in the Bank which was used to exemplify some aspects of social change. The commentary above on Text 3: What a Young Wife Ought to Know ends by suggesting that we need to be careful in making sweeping assumptions about the way our contemporary society is so different from that of previous times.

Research articles and problem pages in various magazines and newspapers to see how they represent relationships between men and women. You could also look at modern examples of self-help books and guides.

SUMMARY

This unit has looked at texts which show attitudes and values in texts which belong to three different genres. In addition to the fact that the genres themselves have changed, each text has been seen to exhibit ideologies which seem different from those we might expect to see represented nowadays. Nonetheless it is important to guard against thinking that these texts represent the views of *all* people at the time they were produced, just as we would not want a single modern text to represent our views. It is equally important to understand that because these texts are in some ways 'old' the ideologies that they present have not necessarily disappeared.

Genre and change

In this unit we will explore how changing social attitudes and practices are reflected within some 'larger' public discourses; in other words we will look at how language change operates within various genres.

GENERIC CONVENTIONS

Some writers may construct texts within generic conventions because they intend their texts to have the particular 'meanings' that are associated with the genre. Readers may interpret such texts according to the same conventions because they are familiar with previous similar texts and recognise the intentions. In other words we read a generic text through an **intertextual** process, using our previous experience of other texts to inform our reading of the current one. So, although genres are in one sense abstract labels without any content as such, in another sense they are very useful in helping us to categorise the vast amount of material we read and hear every day of our lives.

Knowing that readers have previous experience of generic texts allows producers of texts to be confident that they will reach their intended audience(s). This same sense of predictability also allows authors to 'play' with generic conventions and in some way subvert them. A **parody** is a comic variant of a generic text which can be used to amuse, make a satirical point, or both. Advertisements, for example, increasingly use forms of parody to draw our attention to a product or service.

Bex (1996) says that generic labels are used to describe groups of texts which seem to have similar language features and to be performing similar social functions. In other words genres can be analysed from two broad standpoints:

◎ by looking at the linguistic structures in texts;

◎ by looking at the attitudes and values which the texts contain.

Genres as communicative texts indicate what kinds of activities are regarded as important within a society. This means that genres change over time because they reflect the way social situations change. At the same time, by reflecting social change, they can actually reinforce such change. Think, for example, of the ways in which television soap operas have reflected social change since they first appeared on television in the early 1960s, and the ways in which they are 'used' to shape public attitudes to social issues.

Because generic labels are just that, labels without any content as such, it is possible to see language change connecting to genre in three basic ways.

◎ There can be change within a genre, e.g. the way a sports fixture is reported after the event, the way a recipe is written.

◎ There can be a new sub-genre, which belongs to a genre in one sense, but which takes it off in a different direction in another, e.g. a preview of the sports fixture, a celebrity cookery book.

◎ Sometimes the process of generic change goes beyond adapting existing genres, however. New discourse communities may develop with particular interests that are not represented within existing genres. In such cases radically new genres are likely to develop. In addition new genres may develop because new technologies allow new forms of communication, e.g. fans discussing the match in a chat room, recipes on the internet.

Activity

This first activity introduces some practical ways of focusing on genre. Read Text 5: Sincere Male and make notes on the following:

◎ What generic label would you give to this text and where would you expect to find the text?

◎   What language features identify this text as belonging to a genre?

◎   What is the social function of this text?

Text 5: Sincere Male

> **SINCERE male**, 20, 5'8". OHAC and GSH, n/s, WLTM female who likes pubbing, clubbing & keeping fit for friendship, fun and maybe more in future. Genuine replies only please. Call me on Tel _____ .

Commentary

You are unlikely to have had any problems in identifying the genre, although there are different names given to it; these include 'personal ad' and the rather older 'lonely hearts'. In all probability you will have expected to find this text in a newspaper or magazine, especially now that many papers carry the advertisements free of charge. Such ads are also available through text messaging services.

The obvious social function of the text, as it orginally appeared, is to find a partner for the 'sincere male'. In fact, though, it is rather more complex than this. Many people read the personal ads for entertainment rather than to find a new partner. Indeed the writer of the original text seems aware that such advertisements are not always taken seriously – he is 'sincere' and wants 'genuine replies only'. Meanwhile in this book it is serving another purpose again, this time to exemplify a point about genre.

Among the linguistic features which help to place this text, perhaps the most obvious is the information structure. So, for example, you describe yourself first before describing your desired partner, with 'WLTM' acting as the link. Grammatically it is the **ellipsis** that is probably the most apparent. This takes the form of omitted words plus the use of **initialisms** to replace whole phrases. Writing OHAC, for example, cuts space and possibly cost, but depends upon readers knowing that it means 'own house and car'. The creation of verbs – 'pubbing, clubbing' – out of nouns pub/club also saves space and shows how 'new' words can be created by altering a grammatical category. Meanwhile the **pragmatics** of 'maybe more', with its coy avoidance of any direct reference to sex is a typical feature of such advertisements as they appear in mainstream newspapers.

17

SOCIAL FUNCTIONS/LANGUAGE STRUCTURES

What we have seen in the short activity above is that genres can be identified through their social functions and their linguistic structures. If texts serve a social function, then one such function could be that they reflect various social contexts of their time. Clearly there was a time when advertising for a sexual partner was not publicly acceptable, and such advertisements did not exist at all. When they first appeared lonely hearts, as they were then called, were expressed purely in terms of romance rather than having any suggestion of 'anything more'. This suggests that changing attitudes and values around personal and sexual relationships have affected the ways in which personal ads are written.

It should also be noted at this stage that the attitudes and values found in one genre at a specific point in time will also be found in other types of text. So, if the original lonely hearts were coy about sex, then so were romantic stories, films etc.

PROBLEM PAGES

A genre that can be linked to lonely hearts advertisements in that they often appear in similar newspapers and magazines is the problem page. This typically takes the form of a correspondent writing to an 'agony aunt' with a personal problem, and receiving a reply which gives advice on how the problem can be tackled. A variant on this is readers also being invited to reply with their suggestions for help.

In the 'magazine' *Household Words*, founded by Charles Dickens in the nineteenth century, an early example of this genre can be seen in a column which appeared on the back page of each monthly edition and which was entitled *Correspondence*. The page began with a 'Notice to Correspondents' which set out the rules of the column, one of which was as follows:

> That correspondents are urgently requested to adopt distinctive pseudonyms and not to use such vague signatures as 'A Constant Reader' etc.

The rules for the column were followed by a series of 'Answers'. These answers, though, were to questions that were not included in the column.

The following are some of the replies given to people who had presumably used a suitably distinctive pseudonym.

Read the replies shown in Text 6: *Household Words*: Problem Page and make notes on the following:

◎ Make a list of the implied topics that are under discussion, and suggest which are similar to topics in modern problem pages, and which are different.

◎ What are the main features of the narrative voice in these replies? How does it differ from what we expect nowadays?

Text 6: *Household Words*: Problem Page

1. Annie Amour – We are truly sorry for your trouble; at the same time we think you make too much of it. Anyone who would despise you for a defect in your personal appearance would be wholly unworthy of any consideration.

2. E.R.P – the formal reception of company at a court by the Queen or her representative is called Holding a Drawing Room.

3. Fatima – We have not space to discuss the very large subject opened in your letter. We can only recommend you to read history, and getting rid of all prejudices, to decide for yourself where the truth lies.

4. M. Grant – We believe so.

5. Gwendoline – You can hardly call cheese a 'course'. Your dinner would properly be described as three courses.

6. No Relation – It is probably not your fancy, for it has been observed in the case of mature married couples who have lived together for a long period of years, harmonious in thought and feeling, and subject to the same conditions in life, that they acquire a strong facial resemblance.

7. Pomegranate – We will give you the information later on.

8. Ray – The conduct of the gentleman was most reprehensible and rude in the highest degree.

9. Roman Nose – Yes, it is a fact, but not one generally known, that if one holds his breath, wasps, bees and hornets can be handled with impunity.

10. Tom Brown – All we can say is that we are truly sorry for the lady.

11. TJW – Many thanks for your communication. The butter mentioned in the Scriptures is generally supposed to have been a vegetable preparation.

12. TD – We recommend you to try 'Bishop's Granular Effervescent Antipyrin' for your neuralgic pains.

13. WYR – We are requested to state that Miss Amy Levy was an Englishwoman.

(*Household Words*, June 1890)

Commentary

Five main themes can be identified here, although you may well have come up with others. Some replies are in more than one category:

- matters of 'fact' – 9, 11, 13;

- matters of etiquette/manners – 2, 4, 5, 8;

- matters of health advice – 9, 11;

- matters of personal/sexual nature – 1, 6, 8, 10;

- unknown – 3, 4, 7.

Being given only half of the correspondence makes this text highly unusual to modern readers. What exactly was the purpose of the column? Even if it aimed to give information/advice to private individuals writing under pseudonyms, it was still available for all readers who must have been intrigued by what was being referred to. In that sense it was very similar to the modern problem page, where readers' problems are aired in public, perhaps to inform others who have the same problem, but more probably to excite a prurient interest in the misfortune of others.

While some of the questions that were asked can be worked out, others remain vague, either in their content or as to why someone would want to know. Questions 3, 4, 7 are impossible to work out for their content, while 11 is very strange in what it appears to request. Questions 6 and 9 in different ways seem to be giving dubious information as fact – 9 in particular should not be put to the test!

In those replies which seem to indicate 'personal' (i.e. relationship) problems, a very different sense of what is and is not **taboo** is clearly operating here. In 8, for example, just what has the gentleman done? With topics including royal etiquette, facial appearance and the nationality of Miss Amy Levy, the whole nature of what was allowed or expected in public discourse was clearly different then from now.

The unusual and, to modern readers probably rather comic, effect of this column is contributed to by the voice which 'speaks' these answers. Sometimes, as in 4 and 7, it is peremptory. When passing comment, as in 1, 3 and 5, it often seems quite blunt, even rude. We expect public sympathy to be more gentle and forgiving nowadays. The voice is also quite formal in its replies, both in its use of words like 'truly', 'unworthy', 'harmonious' etc., and in its syntax, as in 'Your dinner would properly be described as three courses'.

Household Words was not the only publication giving just answers, as other magazines used this format too, but there were also problem pages which printed both parts of the correspondence.

Text 7: Victorian Magazine: Problem Page is an edited text taken from *Victorian Women's Magazines – An Anthology* edited by Margaret Beetham and Kay Boardman. Read the text and then prepare notes on the following tasks:

1   Comment on the format of this text.

2   What contextual aspects of the text suggest this is not modern.

3   What do you notice about the reply?

(Note: there is a commentary on this activity on p. 100.)

Text 7: Victorian Magazine: Problem Page

CYMON (Sydenham).—'... For two years I have been constant in my attentions to a young lady who gave me every reason to believe my love was returned. Presents have passed between us, and vows of unaltered and unalterable affection ... when visiting the Zoological gardens a week ago I saw a form too well known hanging on the arm of a gentleman, evidently pleased with the attentions he was paying her ... This palpable deception enraged me to the degree that I could not forbear crossing their path and raising my hat said, "Good morning, miss; how do you do?" She immediately gave symptoms of fainting; but I was not to be so taken in, but left her to the care of her sighing swain. I have not seen her since, and do you think I should act rightly in shunning her company for the future?' – We cannot but think that this contretemp might admit a milder construction than CYMON seems to have put upon it. Had the lady no brother or cousin expected from sea, and no acquaintance in the country that required chaperoning around town? However, failing in these suggestions, we advise him to call on the lady, who, no doubt, will easily explain away this slight mistake and all will go merrily as a 'marriage bell'.

SPORTS WRITING

The next part of this unit on genre will look at two texts that are connected in that they are both sports reports, and more specifically that they are both newspaper reports of a football match. The first text is part of a report on the 1882 FA Cup Final between Blackburn Rovers and The Old Etonians. (This report was reprinted in the *Independent on Sunday* in October 2002, but no original source was supplied.) The second text is the opening part of a report in the *Scottish Sun* (17 June 2002) on the World Cup game between Ireland and Spain in Suwon which was won by the Spanish in a penalty shoot-out. ('Penalty shoot-out' is itself a good example of a relatively new lexical item or **neologism** in the sporting vocabulary, comparing a tie-break by penalties to a wild west shooting contest.)

In looking at these two texts, you will be able to see the ways in which a genre has developed and changed over time, yet retained enough features for both texts to be seen as having at least some things in common.

Activity

Read both of the following texts, Text 8A: Blackburn Rovers v Old Etonians 1882 and Text 8B: Republic of Ireland v Spain 2002, and then make notes on the following questions.

- ◎ What similarities can be found in both texts?

- ◎ What differences can be found between the two texts?

- ◎ What reasons can you give for some of the differences?

The commentary can be found after the extracts.

Text 8A: Blackburn Rovers v Old Etonians 1882

Blackburn Rovers   0
Old Etonians   1

AFTER THE strong gales and incommoding rains of the preceding days, the weather broke fair for the final tie for the Football Association Challenge Cup at the Kennington Oval on Saturday afternoon. As three o'clock approached, a large crowd had gathered in the ample arena of the Surrey County Cricket Club, many of them admiring the flat piece of ground that had been staked out in front of the pavilion. Despite the size of the attendance, which experienced witnesses estimated at possibly as big as 6,000, the spectators were good-humoured and the many officials at the ground saw no threat that they would encroach beyond the ropes on to the playing surface. They are fortunate that association football, in the south of the country at any rate, is not cursed with the rowdiness sometimes seen at racecourses.

The match in prospect was an intriguing one, in that it would pit the great Old Etonians, whose name is etched on the Cup along with those of other illustrious sides, among them Old Carthusians, who saw off the Eton challenge last season, against Blackburn Rovers, a team who have, in the past two seasons, secured a reputation for uncompromising play and effective passing. It would be no exaggeration to describe them as the premier side in the north of the country, and, fittingly, they are the first representatives of that territory to reach the final. It would be misplaced, however, to view them as rude mechanicals, for this is not a side drawn, as some northern battalions are, mainly from the labouring classes.

Several of the side are former players at our better public schools and J Brown and the Hargreaves brothers, so prominent in attack and defence for the Rovers, are stalwarts of the England team, one of them participating in last month's 13–0 victory over Northern Ireland at the Knock ground in Belfast. However, there has been, it must be admitted, some talk of the Blackburn club playing men who are recompensed for their efforts, or for the time lost at their employment. We are given to understand that this claim alludes to the Scottish men: McIntyre, who is the landlord of The Castle Inn in Blackburn; Suter, formerly of Darwen and Partick Thistle who works

23

as a tape sizer in the textile trade; and Douglas, the inside-forward and gainer of a Scottish cap, who is employed in a local iron foundry.

However, an account of the Cup's final is not the place to air claims from those who would cast aspersions on these men's amateur status. And so to the match itself. The entry of the two sets of gladiators brought loud cheers from the sidelines, and the Eton team, having won the toss, took up their stations at the western goal ready for the match to be started, which it was, shortly after three o'clock, when Brown of Blackburn set the ball in play. The leather was soon in the possession of the Etonians and they carried the game to the Rovers' territory with clever footwork that resulted in several promising forays and, more than once, a near-successful conclusion.

It was Dunn who finally made the telling move, breaking down the ground with the ball, and passing finally into the goalmouth for Anderson to project it at short range through the posts and give a goal advantage to the southeners. It was a goal the northern supporters thought fortuitous, but it counted nevertheless . . .

Text 8B: Republic of Ireland v Spain 2002

You knocked spots off 'em boys!

IRISH WERE HEROES

SPAIN 1 REP of IRELAND 1
(Spain win 3–2 on penalties)

Bill Leckie in Suwon

KEVIN KILBANE sank to the turf in floods of tears when the reality sunk in – and you just wanted to climb down there and hug him.

He'd missed the kind of open goal every footballer ever born dreams of. He'd had the chance to push his country towards the last eight of the World Cup and had blown it again.

Now he could take no more. And, in front of 40,000 fans and watching millions, he bawled his eyes out.

A backroom man ran to hurl his arms around his waist, squeezing him like a wrestler. Team-mates raced over to tell him everything was all right, that it wasn't his fault.

But right then, no one could convince him. Just like they couldn't convince Matt Holland or David Connolly it wasn't their fault that they'd missed penalties, or Ian Harte's that he'd hit his so weakly in normal time.

Every man out there would think back to one moment when he could have done better.

Gary Breen might have got closer to Fernando Morientes when the cross came in for Spain's goal. Robbie Keane was twice in on keeper Iker Casillas but couldn't lift the ball over him properly either time.

So many ifs and buts and maybes, so long a time ahead of them to wish they could turn the clock back.

Yet the truth is, not one of Mick McCarthy's men could have done any better. The bare facts of who missed what under intense pressure can't take away from the magnificent collective spirit which turned this tie into an all-time classic – not in terms of flowing football or floods of goals but in sheer naked drama.

MATURE

IN THE END they were out, and they were most definitely down, but years from now the real victory will be what this night and indeed this entire tournament does for the nation's game.

Niall Quinn reckons they'll qualify for every big event in the next eight years. I hope so, because there are boys in this squad who deserve to mature on the biggest stage.

And no World Cup or European Championship should ever be without that magnificent green army of fans . . .

Commentary

When comparing texts which span a period of time our attention tends to be drawn to differences, especially if we are comparing an 'old' text with a text that is recently produced. So although there is a temptation to see these two texts as very different – and in some ways they are – because they belong to the same genre there are in fact more similarities than might at first seem to be the case.

Narrative

At the heart of the genre of sports reporting are aspects of representation and **narrative**. Both these texts give a version of events, and they do so using certain narrative methods. These methods are not identical, but they can be seen as having some things in common. So, for example, both can be looked at in terms of their **chronology**.

Text 8A is quite chronologically complex, but it takes an essentially linear approach to time: we begin before the match with a mention of 'the preceding days' and then move towards three o'clock (still incidentally the standard kick-off time for Saturday football matches). There is then a sort of time-out, when for two paragraphs we are taken backwards in time, and the history of the two teams is reviewed. It is here that we see attitudes and values which now seem very dated. Then in paragraph four we move back to the match as it is about to begin. It must be remembered that Text 8A would have been the only source of information on this game – most readers would not even have known the score until they read this story.

Text 8B meanwhile tells its story from a different chronological vantage point – it has to, because virtually all readers will already know the score, and most will have seen the game on television. This text, then, begins just after the game is over, and in the extract here action from the game itself is only mentioned in passing, with a strong suggestion that readers have already seen the action for themselves ('. . . when the cross came in for Spain's goal').

Where the two texts are generically similar, though, is that both do more than give bare information: they both tell a story. This means they can both be analysed by exploring the narrative methods employed. We have already looked at the way time is presented. Another aspect of narrative that can be used is to look at the narrative point of view – where the **narrator**, or voice telling the text, is placed, and what the narratee, or ideal reader hearing the text, is expected to believe. In using the word 'believe' here, it should be clear that narrative point of view involves not only where various elements of the story are positioned, but the attitudes and values which the narrator is assuming the narratee will agree with. Put more bluntly, we can explore the texts for any bias.

Bias

Text 8B clearly positions itself with the Irish team, and expects us to do the same. When we are told 'you just wanted to climb down and hug him' the you is a subtle mixture of the journalist talking about himself and implying that we as readers are involved too. All the drama of the story is from an Irish perspective, with the Spanish barely mentioned. This is what we might expect from a Scottish newspaper, as traditionally many Scots have a close affinity with the Irish.

The position of Text 8A is at first sight harder to define, but if we look at the second and third paragraphs, the ones identified earlier as being outside the chronology of match day itself, we can see some attitudes and values which seem socially outdated now. Any report of a domestic game in a national paper has to be careful about bias, as it might alienate one set of readers, but we can see here that the Old Etonians, who represent southern tradition and good behaviour, are being favoured over Blackburn Rovers who represent both the north and social change. Although care-fully phrased, and often attributed to others, as in 'we are given to under-stand', Blackburn are seen as uncompromising and professional, terms which nowadays could be words of approval but which in this article suggest disapproval.

Discourse structures

Although we have shown aspects of narrative similarity, in terms of **discourse structures** there are some obvious differences, differences which would be found when comparing any newspaper articles across this span of time. So, for example, the anonymous author of Text 8A writes in very long para-graphs and goes to considerable lengths to deny any sense of his own identity. There are no headlines or sub-headings. Text 8B does have a head-line, with a play on the word 'spots' and a colloquial use of ''em'. Bill Leckie uses one or two sentence paragraphs and is happy to identify his own thoughts and hopes as part of the story. There is a clear move from formality to a more informal approach; this is evident in paragraphing, syntax and vocabulary. It is the formality of 'older' texts which often makes them seem so strange on first reading.

Differences can also be found in the football specific vocabulary that is used in the two texts. Text 8A uses terms such as 'took up their stations', 'set the ball in play', 'the leather', 'project it through the posts'. Text 8B has 'hit his (penalty)', 'cross', 'in on keeper'. Interestingly, the **metaphorical** connection between sport and war that is so strong in Text 8A has survived but at the same time has altered in the precise metaphors used. So in Text 8A we have 'gladiators', 'took up their stations', 'territory' and 'forays' and in Text 8B we have 'Mick Mcarthy's men', 'green army of fans', etc.

Conclusion

There are many other features of comparison and contrast which you may have noticed, but on the evidence of these texts the following can be said about changes that occur *within* a genre:

◎   changing social attitudes and values can be seen when comparing texts over time;

◎   levels of formality change with a tendency for modern texts to be more informal;

◎   topic specific vocabulary may change, although it often stays within the same semantic area.

WHAT'S FOR PUDDING?

It has already been noted that there is no scientific basis to genre – generic labels are not fixed and definite points. So whether a text is said to belong to a genre, or to be part of a sub-genre, or indeed to be both, is always open to critical debate. This issue will now be explored further by looking at examples of recipes, more specifically recipes for puddings.

The word 'pudding' has made a considerable shift of meaning over time. Nowadays most people would think of a pudding as a sweet dish, and indeed the word is sometimes used to represent a whole course in a meal – 'what are we having for pudding?'. The word's original meaning, though, can be seen in the way we still refer to 'black pudding' which is essentially a sausage made with blood and fat. Etymologically the word 'pudding' comes from Old French 'boudin' which meant a stuffed intestine.

In her book *Elinor Fettiplace's Receipt Book*, Hilary Spurling (1986) quotes a Frenchman, Henri Misson who, at the end of the seventeenth century, wrote generally disparaging comments about English cooking. When it came to puddings though his tone changed. He wrote:

> Flower, Milk, Eggs, Butter, Sugar, Suet, Marrow, Raisins etc. are the most common ingredients of a *Pudding*. They bake them in an Oven, they boil them with Meat, they make them fifty several ways: BLESSED BE HE THAT INVENTED PUDDING, for it is a Manna that hits the palates of all sorts of people . . . Ah, what an excellent thing is an *English pudding*! *To come in pudding time*, is as much to say, to come in the most lucky Moment in the world . . .

Although Misson does refer to pudding being boiled with meat, from his list of ingredients it would seem that the word 'pudding' by then meant a dish with a 'flower' and suet base.

The recipe below is for 'The Lord of Devonshire His Pudding', taken from *Elinor Fettiplace's Receipt Book* which was compiled by Elinor Fettiplace in 1604 (the word 'recipe' did not come into use until the eighteenth century). Although this book of recipes was copied out by scribes employed for this purpose, it was not intended for wide public scrutiny. Instead such books of recipes and remedies were handed down by gentlewomen from one generation to the next, and then added to by the next in line.

The recipe for this pudding comes under the wider heading of *November*, which would explain Misson's reference above to 'pudding time' – clearly food was much more seasonal than it is now. In addition to being a dedication to an important person, this title also shows a feature of punctuation change. Modern English would say 'Lord Devonshire's pudding', but in the sixteenth century the apostrophe was only just coming into use in English (from French). Some linguistic historians argue that this noun/pronoun/noun pattern as in 'The Lord of Devonshire/His/Pudding' was the origin of the apostrophe to signal possession, with the pronoun 'his' being shortened to 's.

Activity

Read Text 9: The Lord of Devonshire His Pudding, then, bearing in mind your expectations of what a recipe is like generically and the contextual information above, comment on what seem to be the most distinctive aspects of this as a recipe. 'Manchet' is another word for 'bread', literally the finest bread made from wheat flour.

Text 9: The Lord of Devonshire His Pudding

> THE LORD OF DEVONSHIRE HIS PUDDING
>
> *Take manchet and slice it thin, then take dates the stones cut out, & cut in pieces, & reasins of the Sun the stones puld out, & a few currance, & marrow cut in pieces, then lay your sippets of bread in the bottome of your dish, then lay a laying of your fruit & mary on the top, then another laying of sippets of bread, so doo till your dish be full, then take creame & three eggs yolks & whites, & some Cynamon & nutmeg grated, & some sugar, beat it all well together, & pour in so much of it into the dish as it will drinke up, then set it into the oven & bake it.*

Commentary

Some aspects which make this recognisably a recipe are:

◎ it mentions ingredients and what to do with them;

◎ it uses an **imperative** voice – 'Take manchet and slice it thin';

◎ it has a chronological structure working from beginning through to end.

Some aspects you may have noted as unusual are as follows:

◎ Presentationally the recipe does not distinguish between a list of ingredients and the method to be followed. The ornate ampersand (which a computer represents as '&') acts as a discourse marker rather than a connective, sometimes distinguishing between ingredients and sometimes between steps in the method.

◎ The recipe has a vagueness which we would not expect from a modern recipe. How much manchet? How many dates? How big should the dish be? Clearly these were not seen as important – as a cook you would use your eyes, and sense, and get on with it. It must also be remembered that this was not a book for a wide readership, so, unlike modern cookery books, there was no requirement of absolute precision.

◎ There are some unusual ways of describing the food here. 'Manchet' is a specific type of bread, and although we can work out what 'sippets of bread are' we no longer use the term. 'Raisins of the Sun' sounds wonderfully poetic as does the bread drinking up the liquid.

◎ There are various differences from modern spelling, occasional use of capitals, vocabulary that is slightly different from modern use such as 'laying' instead of 'layer'. The phrase 'mary on the top' presumably refers to marrow, which is spelt differently at another point in the text; this shows how spelling was not yet regularised and that different spellings of the same word could appear alongside each other.

Activity

In his book *New British Classics* (2001) Gary Rhodes gives a recipe for 'Bread and Butter Pudding', a dish very similar to the pudding in the activity above. This book was an offshoot of a television series of the same name. Read Text 10: Gary Rhodes' Bread and Butter Pudding, then, bearing in mind the commentary on the recipe by Elinor Fettiplace above, what would you say are the key differences between the two texts, and how would you account for these differences? (Note: the text shown here was also accompanied by a colour picture of the pudding.)

(Note: there is a commentary on this activity on p. 101.)

Text 10: Gary Rhodes' Bread and Butter Pudding

Bread and Butter Pudding

Yet another variation on custard, bread and butter pudding has become one of our classics. It was always a good way of using up stale bread with milk, sugar and eggs, but this would often result in an overcooked, dry and tasteless pud, which left it with a bad name. This recipe will give you quite a different dish, something with an almost sponge-like texture with thick fresh custard oozing out between the layers. I'm using just egg yolks and half milk and double cream which is obviously a little more expensive to make, but once you've tried it you'll never want to make it any other way.

SERVES 6–8

12 medium slices of white bread
50 g (2oz) unsalted butter, softened
8 egg yolks
175 g (6 oz) caster sugar
1 vanilla pod or a few drops of vanilla
   essence
300 ml (½ pint) milk
300 ml (½ pint) double cream
25 g (1 oz) sultanas
25 g (1 oz) raisins

To Finish

Caster sugar

Grease a 1.75 litre (3 pint) pudding basin with butter.

First, butter the bread, remove the crusts and cut in half diagonally, creating triangles. Whisk the egg yolks and caster sugar together in a bowl. Split the vanilla pod, if using, and place in a pan with the milk and cream or add the vanilla essence. Bring the milk and cream to the simmer, then sieve onto the egg yolks, stirring all the time. You now have the custard.

Arrange the bread in layers in the prepared basin, sprinkling the sultanas and raisins in between layers. Finish with a final layer of bread without any fruit on top as this tends to burn. The warm egg mixture may now be poured over the bread and cooked straightaway, but I prefer to pour the custard over the pudding then leave it to soak into the bread for 20 minutes before cooking. This allows the bread to take on a new texture and have the flavours all the way through.

Pre-heat the oven to 180°C/350°F/Gas Mark 4.

Once the bread has been soaked, place the dish in a roasting tray three-quarters filled with warm water. Lightly cover with buttered foil and place in the pre-heated oven. Cook for about 20–30 minutes until the pudding begins to set. Because we are using only egg yolks, the mixture cooks like a fresh custard and only thickens; it should not become too firm.

When ready, remove from the water bath, sprinkle liberally with caster sugar to cover, and glaze under the grill on medium heat. The sugar will dissolve and caramelize and you may find that the corners of the bread start to burn a little. This helps the flavours, though, giving a bittersweet taste, and certainly looks good. The bread and butter pudding is now ready to serve and when you take that first spoonful and place it in a bowl you will see the custard just seeping from the dish. You now have a new British classic at its best.

Note: Freshly grated or ground nutmeg can be sprinkled between the layers for an extra spicy flavour.

The reference above to the way we name meals and courses in meals could become the focus of some wider research on the names given to meals by people of different ages, different regions, different social backgrounds and of different ethnic backgrounds. By use of questionnaires, data could be collected on the variants shown below (this list is not exhaustive though and other variants could be added). The data could then be used to lead to some tentative conclusions about social contexts and language change.

◎ Names for quick meals eaten at any time (i.e. snacks, bait etc.);

◎ names for meals eaten in the middle of the day (i.e. lunch, dinner);

◎ names for meals eaten at various times in the afternoon (i.e. tea, after-noon tea, high tea);

◎ evening meals (i.e. dinner, supper);

◎ names for courses (i.e. sweet, dessert, pudding).

SUMMARY

Thinking in terms of genres which can be explored by looking at both their structures and their ideologies, helps readers to categorise texts. They constantly change, sometimes by dividing into sub-genres, some-times developing into new genres. We have seen, by looking at examples of problem pages, sports writing and recipes, that we can detect different language use and changing social attitudes when we compare texts across time. In particular we have noticed that contemporary texts have a tendency to be more informal than older texts.

33

Interpersonal communication genres and change

In the previous units you were introduced to the idea that language change is inextricably linked to social contexts, generic conventions and ideological attitudes. Changes in language use both express and reflect changes in social practices. In Unit two we looked at texts from commercial publications which involve widespread readership. In this unit we will explore aspects of language change by looking at person-to-person communication produced in private contexts.

WRITING HOME

The first piece of data to be explored in this unit looks at the messages sent on some holiday postcards. Postcards were first used in Britain in 1869. They were a new form of communication in a number of ways: they were 'open' in that the message could be read by anyone; they were pre-paid; they cost less than letters. As with many new forms of communication, they were amazingly popular, with 76 million sent in the first year of their production.

Picture postcards were first produced in Britain in 1902, and Britain was the first country to divide the back of the card to allow both a message and the address. This meant that a holiday postcard, a kind of sub-genre, allowed you to send a picture of where you were and a short greeting.

Holiday postcards have certain generic features, including: they are essentially phatic in purpose, rarely giving any meaningful news or information, and they are often part of a social routine, rather like the sending of Christmas cards. Below are four postcards, two sent in the 1950s and two in the 1990s.

Activity

Look at Text 11: Holiday Postcards. What aspects of interpersonal communication remain constant across the four cards, and in what ways can you say that the two later cards are more informal than the first two? Can you find any other differences between the earlier and later cards?

Text 11: Holiday Postcards

a   Jersey – 1958

Had very enjoyable trip down – up to time – weather above the clouds glorious sunshine. Wet yesterday – fine today but dull. Spent evening with our friends from Durham and met some local people. Bus tour this afternoon so now know a little of the island. 6pm now and sun is shining so hopes are high for the rest of the week. Hotel good and all are well.

Love

Jim and Katie

b   Sidmouth, Devon 1958

Shirley and I are having a lovely holiday here and the weather has been quite good and much warmer than at home. Hope you are well and that we may see you soon. With love from us both.

Lily

c   St Anton, Austria 1998

Have now arrived in St Anton after having a lovely week in Kitzbuhel. The weather has been hot (almost too much for A.) and sunny. Walked for 5 days and cycled for one day – guess which bit felt numb. I'm going to ring you later so you'll have this news before you get it!!

Love Alan and Sheila

Spectacular thunderstorm with lots of lightning last night.

d   West Cork, Ireland 1997

This is the view from a nice bar near our house with live music early evening. Lesley's tanning whilst I study. Nice walks and terrific food – Michael, the local, brings mussels and has just dropped off some pork chops from his just slaughtered pig – that's Ireland.

Rod and Lesley xx

Commentary

While it would be dangerous to generalise about language change on the evidence of only four postcards, cards (a) and (b) have some things in common with (c) and (d), and some things which differ.

All of the cards show the generic tradition of ellipsis by omitting words, although this is most prominent in (a) and they all have terms of approval such as 'enjoyable', 'lovely', 'nice'. The genre does not conventionally allow holidaymakers to say they are having a bad time. All of them refer to the weather, although (d) only does so by implication.

One set of differences is in the way the personalities of the senders (and receivers) are acknowledged much more in the later cards. So there is a saucy reference to sore bums, the fact that some like it hotter than others, some study while other sunbathe, bars are visited and local culture appreciated. These are travellers with little anecdotes they are willing to share, aware that cards serve no real informational purpose at all, especially when they arrive after a phone call. Texts (a) and (b) though are much more formal in the sense that they say so little that is distinctly personal. Note too that (c) adds some late news after signing off. The writer of this card shows a playful awareness of various narrative possibilities, and in that sense is similar to the way some people use emails and chat-rooms.

Extension

1   To explore further some of the issues raised with the postcards above, find your own postcard data. In addition to postcards sent to you, you could also find postcards sold in antique markets or collections belonging to family members.

2   Many electronic postcards are available on-line – a quick search will lead to lots of examples. These postcards and their sites can themselves be researched. It should also be possible to acquire some examples of correspondence in this format, and compare the way people use electronic cards to the way they use the 'real thing'.

FORMALITY AND INFORMALITY

One way in which the written texts above were compared was in their level of formality. It was noted that the two cards sent in the 1990s were more informal in their register. Sharon Goodman (1996) notes that we are living in a time of increased **informalisation**. This word is used to describe the process whereby the language forms that were traditionally reserved for close personal relationships are now used in much wider social contexts such as education, business, politics etc. Referring to the work of Norman Fairclough, she notes: 'professional encounters are increasingly likely to contain informal forms of English; they are becoming in Fairclough's term "conversationalized".'

As with most aspects of language change, attitudes to such informalisation differ (see Unit five for a discussion of attitudes to change). Some would argue that a more informal English in a wide range of contexts breaks down barriers between 'them' and 'us'. Others would argue that the barriers remain, but that we are more liable to be manipulated if they appear not to be.

Text 12: Headmasters' Letters shows two texts with a formality of register which would seem very unusual in contemporary texts, especially when written by two people who are reasonably well-known to each other. As has been stressed throughout this book so far, no simple conclusions about language and time can be made on the evidence of a few short (usually written) texts. The context of the two letters which follow is:

◎ both are men and headmasters as they would have termed themselves, writing in 1953;

◎ they are headmasters of selective schools, O.W. Donaldson of a public school and B.F. Wood of a grammar school (names of people and institutions have been changed);

◎ they have had some social as well as professional contact.

Activity

Read the two letters shown in Text 12: Headmasters' Letters. What features of these letters suggest a high degree of formality compared with what we might expect in a communication nowadays? You could include in your answers reference to:

- ◎ greetings/modes of address;
- ◎ openings and closures;
- ◎ use of vocabulary and **idioms**;
- ◎ attitudes and values that the writers show.

Text 12: Headmasters' Letters

Dear Donaldson

I expect that as soon as you get back to school you will be very busy, so don′.t bother to reply to this letter until things have eased off.

I am trying to persuade my Ladies Working Party not to present the school with a sound film projector (price about £200) for Coronation Year, but to let us have a tape recorder (very much cheaper) instead, in the hope that they might let us use the difference for certain other purposes near to my heart.

Despite my efforts, they still remain unconvinced as to the value of a tape recorder as against a sound film projector. I have told them that what worries me is that I may not be able to use a sound projector as much as they think I should. They insist, quite rightly, that they want something that every child in the school can enjoy and participate in.

You I know have a tape recorder which you value highly. Am I looking a gift horse in the mouth and being rather silly about things? What do you think I should do – accept the sound film projector and be thankful or try to re-inforce my suggestion for a tape recorder?

With kind regards,

Yours sincerely,

BFW

Dear Wood,

Before I waver in the decision you have asked me to make – the advice you asked me to give – let me say firmly (I shall regret this later) that I should go for the sound film projector. This is clearly a thing you will never regret having and it will open the way to a greater number of films etc. at your discretion and it will be difficult at any time to lay your hands on such a sum of money as would be needed. On the other hand, while the tape recording machine is expensive, round about £70, it might not be impossible to raise this money – or again, the price may well come down within a year or two.

Put it how you like, while the recorder would be of immense interest and value, I think it probably your duty to have the sound projector as a school possession. These days a headmaster can hardly hold his head up if he has to confess a lack of such a thing!

We must meet soon and talk about Italy. I was very glad to get your card.

Kindest regards to you both

Yours sincerely

O W Donaldson

Commentary

When considering aspects of change over time, it is worth bearing in mind the modes of communication available when the text was produced, and the means by which the physical text itself was produced. In 1953 two options were available to Wood – he could write a letter, which he would almost certainly have dictated to his female secretary or he could have made direct contact with his colleague by telephone. It should be remembered though that in those days the telephone was not used lightly or frequently.

It is hard to imagine letters like this being written nowadays. Did people really write at such length about such trivia? Did headmasters have nothing better to do? Nowadays a quick email, or phone call would surely do the trick. The letters here seem formal and distant – perhaps because they are accessed by the secretaries doing the typing and so the writers are aware that the letters are not strictly personal.

The formality, especially in the first letter, is because there is so little sense of the sort of 'conversational' writing that we are used to now. There is the contraction 'don't' in the rather odd first paragraph, and occasional uses of dashes and questions, but the careful organisation and precise structuring of 'Despite my efforts, they still remain unconvinced as to the value of a tape recorder as against a sound film projector' sound very stiff and formal. Indeed the consistent failure of Mr Wood to shorten the noun phrase 'sound film projector' is unusual for modern ears, but can possibly be accounted for by the fact that a model suitable for schools was a recent invention at that time. (Mr Donaldson does contract the phrase once to 'sound projector' and in the process shows off that he is a bit more aware of modern technology.) The way the two 'friends' address each other by their surnames also sounds strange now, when first names are so much more common.

Both letters begin unusually for modern readers, although perhaps here there are attempts by both men to sound relaxed and informal. The closures, though, are different from each other. Wood asks a series of questions which he wants answering, Donaldson makes a gesture towards something more social – although it is very tentative. Both letters conclude with the routines of formal letter writing, although the respective secretaries have different views on how to punctuate them.

The term 'idiom' refers to commonly used expressions which are usually metaphorical in structure. Because they are not literal in their meanings, idioms can have a limited life span. Expressions such as 'near to my heart', 'look a gift horse in the mouth', 'hold his head up' which might have sounded quite informal when used, now seem dated.

There are a number of attitudes and values which can be seen here. Some involve gender such as the use of the term (and the existence of the organisation) 'Ladies Working Party' and the implication that only men (i.e. 'headmasters') run schools. Meanwhile these senior schools have children not students. There also seems to be something rather sly and conspiratorial going on here: what are the 'certain purposes', and does Wood really want the tape recorder for himself? He is told it is his duty and the fashion to have a projector, not that it is actually a good thing educationally. The expression of personal desire seems constrained by the format of the letter and the nature of the relationship between the two men.

TELEPHONE VOICES

One obvious vehicle for spoken communication which is not face-to-face is the telephone. Hopper (1992) has identified the following pattern of opening routines which often, but not always, take place in land-line telephone calls. (The routine can alter depending upon various contexts.) In doing this he shows that in conventional phone conversations greetings are not the first exchange when people talk, as they are in face-to-face conversations.

1   There is a summons–answer sequence in which the ring is the caller requesting to speak to the answerer, which is followed by the answerer saying that they are responding i.e.:

> *Caller*:   Ring ring ring (usually up to about 30 seconds if there is no reply).
> *Answerer*: Hello.

This means that it is the responder to the call who speaks first.

2   This is then followed by identification/recognition sequences where the answerer is identified i.e.:

> *Caller*:   Is that Mary?
> *Answerer*: Speaking.

3   There is then a greeting sequence, consisting of what Hopper calls 'greeting tokens' which also includes the self-identification of the caller i.e.:

> *Caller*:   Hi, this is Robert.
> *Answerer*: Hi Robert.

4   This is followed by what Hopper calls 'initial enquiries' e.g.:

> *Caller*:   How are you?
> *Answerer*: Fine, and you?

In this form of exchange the use of 'hello' at the start is not a greeting as such. It is when the speakers in the above example say 'hi' that the real greeting takes place, followed by the initial enquiries of 'how are you'. These, of course, are not really literal enquiries. It may well be that speakers have had terrible days, but they will still often say that they are fine, especially with people they do not know very well.

The increasing sophistication of telephone technology, though, produces changes in the routines described above. Mobile phones, number identification systems and video conference calls, where people can see each other, are all introducing different openings to telephone conversations. For example, where phones have caller display, the person answering the phone will often begin by naming and greeting the caller. With mobile phones it is then the *location* of the answerer which is often what is in doubt. When we overhear people stating what to us is the obvious – 'I am on the train' – this is not obvious to the caller. Another thing to notice about mobile phone use is that we are often conducting private phone calls in public places, and that people speaking on mobile phones behave very differently from when they are in public face-to-face conversations. Such behaviours can be seen as examples of language change within a broader social context.

Activity

1 Research ways you and your friends conduct opening exchanges on mobile phones. What patterns of openings/greetings can you detect?

2 Transcribe a series of messages left on an answerphone. What patterns of language use can you find? How are the replies affected by the invitation to leave a message?

(Note: there is no commentary for this activity.)

MULTIMODAL COMMUNICATION

From a perspective of language change **multimodal** forms of communication, such as emails, text messages and chat-rooms, are essentially new forms of communication. As used here the term 'multimodal' refers to the way that texts use devices from a range of different communication systems at the same time. So, for example, you can send an email message to six of your friends simultaneously; previously you could only do this through speaking to them as a group. In other words writing takes on a characteristic which once belonged to speech only.

Earlier in this unit reference was made to electronic postcards being available on-line. In many ways these electronic media are nothing like postcards at all, yet they retain through their name a metaphorical connection with an older form of communication. A similar process can be seen in many aspects of computer terminology which operates in what Shortis (2001) calls 'a virtual environment of extended imagery'. So, as we move on to consider some aspects of emails, it is worth pausing to consider the visual and verbal imagery which surrounds us when we communicate in this way.

EMAILS

Although most of us now spell the word 'email' and are happy to use it as a verb – we email our friends – the noun was originally spelled 'e-mail' which stood for 'electronic mail'. The American 'mail' is used instead of the British 'post'. The icon we click on to start the programme is an envelope, and we also see opened envelopes when we 'receive' our mail. We have address books to consult, and our mail comes into our 'inbox'. In other words, the virtual reality of cyberspace mail is constructed by a set of words and images which suggest the old-fashioned postal service (or mail) that preceded it. The same sort of process can be seen in the office metaphors that dominate our computer 'desktop'. When we send a copy of a mail, for example, we 'Cc' it, these letters standing for 'carbon copy'; we throw our rubbish in the waste-basket, or in newer programs the recycling bin, showing that virtual offices have to care for the environment too.

Activity

Look through the most recent emails you have sent/received. Can you find any patterns in the way you greet/address people and the way they greet/address you? You could, for example, tabulate numerically the number of times a certain greeting is used, whether there are differences of use across social areas such as age and gender, and where there is no greeting at all.

Commentary

There are clearly no right answers here, but most people's email correspondence will contain a whole range of greetings formats. The following are some examples:

◎   no greeting at all

◎   just an initial e.g. A

◎   first name

◎   Dear + first name

◎   Hi

◎   Hi + first name

◎   Hi there

◎   nickname

◎   Hello

◎   Hello + first name

The situation can be slightly altered if you are sending a reply by using the 'reply to mail' format. In this case contact has already been established and you are in one sense continuing a dialogue that has already started. These exchanges could be called **adjacency pair** messages, in that they have a clear structure. It should also be remembered that when you receive an email you are told who it is from and what it is about, and so the communication has already started before you open your mail.

What can be seen from the list above is that it is very unusual to find the sort of formal greetings structures that characterise official letters when looking at email. Indeed there are times when it is quite hard to know how to start an email, if you are writing to someone who has more power than you. Over-formality can appear sycophantic, overfamiliarity rude. So, although it is possible to say that emails are usually less formal than written letters, you still have to get the pragmatics right in this mode of communication. As with all social encounters, getting the pragmatics right is crucial to success. The unwritten rules of 'netiquette' can be as tricky as those of any other communication medium.

Extension

Read Text 13: Emails which show an exchange of emails between two colleagues, Liz and Alan. They have arranged a meeting for 18 October, where Liz is going to present some documents to Alan. You have already looked at the two letters from the 1950s (in Text 12: Headmasters' Letters) using the following sub-headings:

◎   aspects of formality/informality;

◎   modes of address;

◎   openings and closures;

◎   use of idioms;

◎   attitudes and values.

Now use the same sub-headings to analyse the following texts. At the same time consider the purpose of each of the two emails and what it tells you about the relationship between Liz and Alan.

Text 13: Emails

Dear Alan

Im humming and haaing abt Fri 18th. I think Ian will be coming to the the meeting but I shd be able to meet you later IF done anything constructive which is a big if at the moment. Im certianly aiming to have a piece to submit but at present feels like Everest to climb havent even started redraft due to crazy psycho witch at work (I have my own stalker!!! calling me for an hour or more at home in the evenings!!) plus additional wall to wall crap. Not making preemptive excuse but forewarning. Hope this temporary glitch only – I swear on my life that if I thought I couldnt deliver the thing at all wld tell you up front so you cld get someone else! So am hoping not to welsh on our deal but feel honourbound to tell you might HAVE to delay past 18th Oct. V embarrassed as I know I suggested this date. Mortified. Dont miss deadlines ever – vv bad sign.

Hope you're ok

Liz

Hi Liz

No need to panic – not sure I can make it anyway. Would rather re-programme to Nov 4. Any good?

A

Commentary

The emails are clearly not identical in their forms of address: for example Liz begins with a traditional 'Dear Alan', he replies 'Hi Liz'. Note though that first names are used here, not the surnames used in Text 12: Headmasters' Letters. (The fact that this is a mixed sex exchange could also be a factor here.) Note also that the greetings/address are placed traditionally at the top of the text and separated from the body by a space. She signs off with 'Liz', although she will have been identified more fully at the top of the email. Alan just puts 'A' – when using 'reply to sender' he needs to do no more.

Liz has made no effort to paragraph her mail, nor has she corrected the many 'mistakes' that she makes. She uses various graphological devices which also help to break down the formality of the mail – e.g. capital letters, abbreviations, exclamation marks, brackets. She also uses a range of sentence structures, which include single words, elliptical phrases and very long compounds. The effect of this is to make the writing sound as if it is being spoken – exactly the opposite of the letters from the 1950s.

This idea of the text sounding as if it is spoken needs to be taken a bit further though because it is not really like a conversation as such. Instead it is a text 'spoken' by a sort of multi-voiced persona, a persona who at times dithers, at times rambles, at times gets on with it. Where there are some aspects of formal vocabulary included – 'preemptive', 'forewarning', 'honour-bound' – they sound as if they have been included as deliberate comic contrast to the more idiomatic language. What is really seen here is a literary construction of created voices. This is a form of 'play' (in both senses of the word) that is absent from the two headteachers' letters. They too acted out a role in their writing, but it was a consistent role, without any apparent sense of irony.

David Crystal in *Language and the Internet* (2001) refers to the 'dialogic character of e-messaging'. The word **dialogic** is used to suggest that many emails are part of an *exchange* of communications, in the way that traditional letters often were not. (The letters from the two headteachers, seen above, which do form part of an exchange, lack the sense of immediacy of reply that is possible with emails.) Crystal claims that it is the dialogic nature of emails which is more significant than the lexical informality. Note, though, that although Liz sounds as though she is speaking her text, what she writes is very different from what she would actually say. Her rapid delivery and constant switch of topic would leave any listener bewildered.

Liz uses many idiomatic terms, including 'psycho witch at work', 'wall to wall crap' and 'temporary glitch'. These could again be used for comic effect. Additionally the use of 'vv bad sign' may be a deliberate intertextual echo of Bridget Jones. So what Liz is doing here is inventing a dramatic persona for herself, as a woman who may fail to deliver on a task because the world is treating her unkindly.

Alan's reply is much briefer and gets quickly to the main issue. But then in this case he does seem to have the power. However we read Liz's 'performance' – and we can only guess at how well the two people know each other – there seems to be a sense in which Alan is right when he talks of 'panic'. Liz does indeed seem desperate to justify herself.

Liz uses what conversational analysis researchers calls a 'pre-closing formula' when she puts 'Hope you're ok' on a separate line. Alan does not use any pre-closures in his reply.

TEXT MESSAGES

Just as the invention of the postcard led to a massive usage, so has the advent of text messages. 70 per cent of all mobile phone users also use text messaging, and, in 2002, 16.8 billion messages were sent in the UK alone (according to figures from the Mobile Data Association). This figure will almost certainly continue to rise year by year. SMS (short message system) communication, as a new form of communication, can be approached by linguists in various ways. One obvious way is to look at the language used in an 'internal' or technical way. So, for example,

> :-0 HBTU 0-:

can stand to represent 'singing Happy Birthday to you'. In this message there are:

◎ emoticons, which are, at the stretch of the imagination, **iconic** representations of an action or emotion;

◎ initials in **collocation** standing for the first letters of a well-known phrase (happy birthday to);

◎ a letter homophone 'u' standing for 'you'.

DON'T BE L8 or LUV J have further conventions such as:

◎ a number homophone '8' for 'l-*ate*';

◎ a 'phonetic' spelling of the word 'luv'.

49

Although various magazines and websites often suggest that such technical conventions are standardised, and so print lists of text message 'words', new inventions are being made all the time. One reason for the conventions is that there are only 160 characters available to use, and the physical act of texting can take time. Evidence shows, though, that most messages are much shorter than this anyway, so space is not really the main issue. It would appear that inventing new ways of saying often quite banal things is part of the fun of the process: that texting is so popular because of its incentives to be playful and inventive.

This leads to a second way of looking at the language of texting. This involves a wider consideration of the medium itself and the contexts within which it is used. Unlike mobile phone use, especially in public places, it is private, which allows messages to have a number of purposes and effects. If over 16 billion messages are sent a year, what is there to say that was going unsaid previously? The private nature of the medium means messages can be silly, sexy, informational and, above all, making contact – keeping a channel of communication open and having fun in the process. Or, on the down side, the private nature of the medium means it is said to be ideal for bullies, stalkers, criminal gangs etc.

A third approach is to look at attitudes to the medium and language that is used. As with all activities associated especially with the young, it has led to great concern over declining standards of behaviour, especially with regard to language use. So, for example, when it was disclosed that a student had written in text message form in an English GCSE exam, there was universal outrage, and dire forecasts of a complete deterioration in all formal standards of writing. What has tended to be overlooked in this debate is that text messages are a new genre, and as with all genres, it has its own conventions, limitations and boundaries which make it inappropriate to judge against the standards of formal standard written English. (See Unit five for more on attitudes to language.)

Finally, it must be remembered that behind new technological genres lies big business forever searching for the 'next' new craze to make lots of money. With each subtle shift in the voice/text/time relationship, a new genre will lead to new ways of communicating.

Using the three approaches to text messaging outlined above, you could do one or more of the following research tasks:

1   Collect some data and analyse the technical methods used. You could refine this further by seeing whether different groups, such as age groups, use different conventions.

2   Collect data from a number of sources and present some statistical data based on the apparent purposes of the messages sent. Remember that each message may well have more than one purpose.

3   Conduct some research on usage and attitudes to texting. Question-naires could be used to find out who uses text messaging, and what attitudes there are to the language that is used.

(Note: there is no commentary for this activity.)

CHAT-GROUPS

Whereas emails are usually message exchanges between a pair of named individuals communicating on a single issue, chat-groups usually involve several people: they can be anonymous or use a pseudonym; their communication can be of an indefinite length; and they can cover a wide range of topics. Crystal (2001) uses the term 'asynchronous' to describe groups where 'postings' are placed on 'boards' and 'synchron-ous' to describe groups who 'chat' in real time. The terms 'email' and 'text message' both suggest a written form, but the terms 'chat-room/ chat-group' suggest a form of talk; a form of talk – chat – that is tradi-tionally seen as social rather than serious in its content.

Although the terminology that labels new communication genres draws upon the traditional binary opposites of speaking/writing (mail/ chat), it is not very helpful to see such texts as products of these oppo-sites. Instead each of the genres has its own unique methods of communication, and then each of the texts produced within the genre has its own specific context. So, for example, the idea of turn-taking, which is crucial to many kinds of vocalised talk, is achieved in very different ways in chat-groups. The acts of reading, thinking, replying and sending the reply, which is not necessarily received instantly, is being undertaken by each of the participants at the same time. This inevitably leads to a dislocation of the exchange in a way that does not happen with emails and text messages. Yet participants within the process are well able to manage this complicated exercise in pragmatics.

Another aspect of pragmatics involves the fact that whereas in face-to-face group conversation your presence is still registered, even if you are silent, this is more problematic in chat-groups. As Crystal (2001) notes: 'in chatgroups silence is ambiguous: it may reflect a deliberate withholding, a temporary inattention, or a physical absence (without signing off).'

Activity

Text 14: Chat-group Log involves university students, who, as part of their Communication course, were expected to communicate with Swedish students via IWD – Interactive Written Discourse, which is a more specific term for the more general term 'chat'. Because this was part of a course in Communication, rather than a commercial chat-room open to anyone, the participants used their real names, and to some extent knew each other already. They were also aware that their tutor had access to their 'chat'.

Make notes on what you notice about this data, in particular looking at the ways in which topics are managed by the participants.

(Note: there is a commentary on this activity on p. 101.)

Text 14: Chat-group Log

```
Becca Wood>>heloo
Rosie Wayman>>fancy meeting you in here
Becca Wood>>i hate this cos I never know what to say
Rosie Wayman>>what do you think of this part of the card
Rosie Wayman_#2>>course I mean course
Becca Wood>>oh right
Becca Wood>>I don't know, I'm not sure yet
Rosie Wayman_#2>>daunting
Becca Wood>>very
Becca Wood>>it's different and interesting but I don't have a
clue what I'm meant to be doing
Rosie Wayman_#2>>snap
Becca Wood>>have you started your psychology essay yet
(changing the subject a little)
->->->->Andrew Turner connected at: Tue Feb 22 2000 10:56:59
Rosie Wayman>> the hole language barrier scares me and what if
```

I have nothing to say
Becca Wood>>I know what you mean, i can say I love you in
swedish, but I don' think that will be very useful
->->->->Andrew Turner disconnected at: Tue Feb 22 2000
10:57:39
Rosie Wayman_#2>>no I haven't started my essay, i have loads
of books but i need another one before I start
Becca Wood>>same here
Rosie Wayman_#2>>i love you i can't say anything
Becca Wood>>actually it might be norwegen, which i can say i
love you in
Rosie Wayman_#2>>do you understand the essay questions
Becca Wood>>i tend to talk rubish, i'm sorry, i've got
wafflyitus
->->->->Jennifer Kirk connected at: Tue Feb 22 2000 10:59:12
Becca Wood>>i understand it ish, but i still have no idea what
to write
Jennifer Kirk>>hel l l l l l l l l l loooooooooooooo
Becca Wood>>hi there
Rosie Wayman_#2>>as a child I was taught french welsh and
german and now I have a right mix so I have given up
Becca Wood>>how's it goin Jen
Jennifer Kirk>>not tooooooo bad
Rosie Wayman_#2>>hi Jen
Jennifer Kirk>>hiya
Becca Wood>>can you speak fluently in those
Rosie Wayman_#2>>have you done the essay
Rosie Wayman_#2>>I cant even count to ten
Jennifer Kirk>>I haven't even started the essay yet
whooooops !
Becca Wood>>oh
Becca Wood>>neither have i
Jennifer Kirk>>I am going to start this aft and finish it
tomorrow. i have done some reading
Rosie Wayman_#2>>i don't know what else t a
Becca Wood>>i hate these silly machines, I never know what to
say, at least I know you lot, but what happens when the
Sweedish people are in here too, i'll look a propper banana
Rosie Wayman>>omueril
Rosie Wayman_#2>>cpt lcomputer ill
Becca Wood>> what
Jennifer Kirk>>eh
Rosie Wayman>>oh its ok again now
Rosie Wayman_#2>>mad
Becca Wood>>i'm going to leave you for a while to see if i've
got any e-mails from my friends see ya
<-<-<-<-<- Becca Wood disconnected at: Tue Feb 22 2000
11:03:50
Jennifer Kirk>>byyyyeeeeee I'm off!!!!!!
<-<-<-<-<- Jennifer Kirk disconnected at: Tue Feb 22 2000
11:04:06
Rosie Wayman_#2>>see you

Extension

1   Using letters as a generic model you could:

   ◎   study various types of letters sent over an extended period of time;

   ◎   look at the stylistic methods of one letter writer;

   ◎   compare 'older' letters with more modern ones;

   ◎   compare 'posted' letters with emails.

2   It was noted above that there are considerable variant possibilities within the medium of emails. You could produce a quantitive study of such variables which might include:

   ◎   greetings;

   ◎   forms of address;

   ◎   pre-closures;

   ◎   replies and how people respond to the original mail;

   ◎   accuracy in spelling;

   ◎   stylistic range across emails sent by one person;

   ◎   the significance of context for both sender and receiver.

3   Consider the pragmatics involved in interpersonal communication within a 'new' genre.

SUMMARY

This unit has built upon the earlier work on genre by looking at some genres used when people communicate person-to-person without being face-to-face and it has noted a tendency towards a growing informalisation in such communication. It has also looked at multimodal forms of communication and in particular focused on the way participants are able to both use and play with the new methods of communication.

Visual representation and change

SEMIOTICS AND REPRESENTATION

The word 'representation' is an important term in the study of communication. It is used to distinguish between what is 'real' and how such 'reality' is presented and labelled. At a simple level we can say that the word 'book' is a label for what you are reading now, but it is not the actual thing itself. This means that language is an arbitrary system, in that it is made up of culturally agreed connections between words and meanings. 'Book', we agree if speaking English, means an object with pages and words that we read, but there is nothing in the series of letters 'b o o k' which says it *has* to mean this.

In **semiotics**, or the study of how we read **signs**, two basic elements of meaning can to be distinguished. The **signifier** is the actual marks on the page (in this case the word 'book'), the **signified** is what the marks on the page can be seen to represent (in this case an object with pages and words, something which is usually deemed to be of intellectual value). It is important to understand at this point that the signified is not fixed – it can mean different things to different people in different cultures at different times, which is of particular relevance to the topic of this book.

In looking at texts from a perspective of language change, therefore, an important aspect to look at is the way visual representation works in the texts. In terms of the signifiers in texts, it is possible to comment on such things as typographical variation, approaches to layout etc. These visual elements will differ depending on the genre of text we are looking at: poems will be printed in lines and perhaps stanzas; advertisements are likely to have logos, photos, illustrations, different sizes and types of font; web pages will have hyperlinks and image buttons to click on. It is important to remember, though, that content and form are inextricably linked – the visual elements of a text are part of its meaning structure, not, somehow, an addition to it.

It is the signified aspects of texts which lead to the more interesting analysis, however, because the meanings which can be found will involve an awareness that the texts had a cultural context at their time of production which is almost certainly different from the current one. The attitudes and values in 'old' texts are not always going to be the same as those held now.

Note: for a fuller exploration of this important area, see Unit one of the core book in this series *Working with Texts*.

Activity

Imagine you are asked by a child to draw a picture of an elephant for him or her. Have a go at what you would draw. When you have done this, label the drawing with a human quality that the elephant is said to possess.

What can you learn from this process about aspects of visual representation?

(Note: there is a commentary on this activity on p. 103.)

GRAPHEMIC SYMBOLS

The previous activity has looked at some aspects of the visual representation of an object, in this case an elephant. In similar ways the writing system we use in English can be used to represent certain meanings. Sharon Goodman (1996) notes that the letter 'X' (upper-case; 'x', lower-case), which appears infrequently in written words, is in fact a 'supercharged typographic icon'. The signifier X is a **graphemic symbol** and is used to create a whole range of signified meanings. One example is that it is can be used to represent a kiss.

1   Make a list of other ways in which the letter 'x' can be used, beyond
     its use in the spelling of conventional words, and the meanings which
     are attached to it. Then consider which uses of 'x' are long standing
     and others that are more recent.

2   In what ways are other letters used as graphemic symbols?

(Note: there is a commentary on this activity on p. 104.)

FINDING MEANINGS IN VISUAL REPRESENTATION

From the earliest writing and then printing, meanings have been
contributed to by the way a text looks and by visual signs contained
within the text. Indeed the very first evidence of human communication that we have, cave drawings and paintings, are complex representations of the cave dwellers' lives. Illustrated bibles, handwritten
by monks, contain elaborate drawings, and the first printed books
contain a variety of fonts and designs. It is almost impossible to find a
text that does not in some way have a visual element contributing to its
meanings.

Text 15: Shakespeare Dedication forms the second page of an edition of the
poem 'Venus and Adonis' written by William Shakespeare and published by
Richard Field in London 1593. The text is a dedication of the poem to the
author's patron, The Earl of Southampton, who essentially paid Shakespeare
so that he could write. Following the text is a transliteration, so that it
can be read more easily. Spelling and grammar are as in the orginal, but
some letters have been changed to give them their modern appearance:
so, vv = w, ʃ = s, u = v in some cases.

◎   What is the main purpose of this text?

◎   What visual features of the text contribute to its main purpose?

◎   What other aspects of language change can you see in this text?

Text 15: Shakespeare Dedication

TO THE RIGHT HONORABLE
Henrie VVriothefley, Earle of Southampton,
and Baron of Titchfield.

Ight Honourable, I know not how I shall offend in dedicating my vnpolisht lines to your Lordship, nor how the worlde vvill cenfure mee for choofing fo ftrong a proppe to fupport fo vveake a burthen, onelye if your Honour feeme but pleafed, I account my felfe highly praifed, and vowe to take aduantage of all idle houres, till I haue honoured you vvith fome grauer labour. But if the firft heire of my inuention proue deformed, I fhall be forie it had fo noble a god-father : and neuer after eare fo barren a land, for feare it yeeld me ftill fo bad a harueft, I leaue it to your Honourable furuey, and your Honor to your hearts content, vvhich I wifh may aluuaies anfuuere your ovune vvifh, and the vvorlds hope full expeftation.

Your Honors in all dutie,

William Shakefpeare.

TO THE RIGHT HONORABLE
Henrie Wriothesley, Earle of Southampton
and Baron of Titchfield

Right Honourable, I know not how I shall offend in
dedicating my unpolisht lines to your lordship, nor
how the worlde will censure mee for choosing so
strong a proppe to support so weake a burthen,
onelye if your Honour seeme but pleased, I ac-
count my selfe highly praised, and vowe to take advantage of all
idle houres, till I have honoured you with some graver labour. But
if the firste heire of my invention prove deformed, I shall be sorie it
had so noble a god-father: and never after care so barren a land,
for feare it yeeld me still so bad a harvest, I leave it to your Honourable surucy, and your Honour to your hearts content, which I wish
may alwaies answere your owne wish, and the worlds hopefull expectation.

Your Honors in all dutie
William Shakespeare

Commentary

This text is designed as a piece of flattery. The author assumes the role of a
worthless writer who is not worthy of his patron. In role, he grovels to his
superior – the strong prop (i.e. Southampton) is not needed to support such
a weak burden (i.e. the pathetic poem Shakespeare pretends he has written).
A dedication such as this is predicated upon the fact that the writer is at the
economic mercy of the patron. We assume now, and presumably readers
knew it then too, that this is a conventional role play. Although modern texts
often contain acknowledgements, if they were written like this they would
be seen as horribly shallow and grovelling (or perhaps a joke). An obvious
clue to the flattery involved here is the number of times the word
'Honourable' and its associated forms is used.

The text uses a number of visual elements to support its purpose. The
ornate heading is an intricate pattern, suggesting something or someone of
importance. In other words there is a semiotic significance in the typography.
Different font sizes are then used to name the patron, with the first line in
block capitals. The ornate R in a large box accompanied by a flowery pattern
is traditional way of writing the first letter of a text, but it does not have a

symbolic value in the way we have previously seen that letters can have. The use of a form of italics highlights the fact that this is not the poem itself but an addition to it.

There are a number of ways in which this text shows that 'rules' of writing were not yet fully established. So, for example, the gaps after punctuation marks are irregular, possessive apostrophes are not used, word order is sometimes inverted ('I know not'), spelling is often unusual to a modern eye, some words seem to have an unfamiliar usage ('onelye' would seem to mean 'but' and 'surucy' perhaps meaning something like 'surety') and the grammar of the long last sentence makes it hard to follow, even if a general sense can be found.

VISUAL SOPHISTICATION

Over recent time in particular, the process of visual representation has become a more sophisticated process with an increasing demand on the reader to make cultural connections from a wide range of complex semiotic signifiers. While we might in the past have expected to see this when reading a comic, or certain newspapers, or advertisements for commercial products, there would have been an expectation that more 'serious' texts would consist of largely formal, densely printed text, with relatively little visual variation. Although such texts are still plentiful enough in certain contexts – think for example of the legal statements that form the the literal and metaphorical 'small print' – many informative and/or persuasive texts are nowadays more likely to have a much greater level of visual sophistication.

Activity

Look back at the following texts which appeared in Unit one of this book, and consider the extent to which visual representation is an important part of the way the texts are read:

◎ Text 1: A Career in the Bank

◎ Text 2: The Kid-Glove Collier

◎ Text 3: What a Young Wife Ought to Know

◎ Text 4: Bank of Scotland Investment Service Recruitment

(Note: there is no commentary for this activity.)

The increasing sophistication noted above is also in part a result of technological advances which allow more complex processes of text production. Recent advances in 'new' technologies take this a step further; anyone with a computer and a little knowledge can produce their own texts, make their own website etc. In doing so they will almost certainly use a wide variety of visual representation to contribute to their meanings. This visual representation will almost certainly contain examples of graphics, pictures, layout techniques as well as words themselves – and the words will almost certainly be written in a variety of typefaces which can be altered at the click of a mouse.

VISUAL REPRESENTATION IN MULTIMODAL TEXTS

As Sharon Goodman (1996) points out 'texts in English, are becoming increasingly multimodal – they use devices from more than one semiotic mode of communication simultaneously'. In other words, texts increasingly no longer rely on words alone – they contain words, pictures, images etc. taken from a range of fields of communication. In addition written texts often incorporate representations of spoken forms – texts 'speak' to us in a much more direct way.

The recognition of multimodality in texts has led some educationalists to suggest that children need to be taught visual literacy as well as the literacy involved in decoding plain written text. Goodman also notes that finding a term to describe the visual elements of a text is problematic. She asks the following questions:

Can we say that any picture or graphic representation accompanying English words may be called 'visual English'?

Does the move towards the visual entail a move away from distinct 'languages' – in other words is the 'Englishness' of English texts disappearing?

Certainly the analysis of the visual elements of texts is not the work of students doing English alone. Students of art, art history, communications, psychology, history, media and no doubt other subjects too could all analyse the same texts from slightly different theoretical starting points.

Text 16: Intertext Advertisement shows a web page advertising the Intertext series. Although produced here in black and white, if you go to the address (www.routledge.com/rcenters/linguistics/series/intertext/titles.html) you will find a colour version.

What reading skills are required to make use of this text?

Text 16: Intertext Advertisement

This text works by offering the reader choices which lie 'behind' what is given here. So, for example, we are currently in the page 'series titles', and we can next go off in various directions, depending upon our requirements, which could be to search for something specific, or which could be to browse more generally. On the left we are given alternative general categories, on the right we are given further choices within this category.

Written text has in the past been traditionally linear, as is the case with this book. 'Linear' in this sense means that the text follows a line, and to some extent the success of this book will be if the readers find it easy to follow the arguments in a sequential way. Clearly the web page does not work in this way though, partly of course because web 'pages' are not pages in the original sense at all – whereas in traditional texts we turn the page to find out what happens next, web pages offer us different reading routes. We are, though, expected to understand how such web pages work – this one assumes we know what a 'home' page is, and that the links to the specific book titles are 'live'.

In addition to being non-linear, this page is also typical of certain web pages in that we are given bite-sized information or instructions, rather than extended stretches of language. (The term 'bite-sized' playfully recognises two meanings of the word 'bite'.) A recognition that we are not meant to read this page in the way we would read a book can be seen in the way the designers of the page have aligned the text to the right of the column of book titles, rather than to the traditional left. You may also have spotted yet another appearance of the letter 'x ' in the banner at the top of the page.

This web page could be seen as essentially verbal, in that it largely uses words, but it clearly requires a different sort of literacy from, say, reading a novel, if it is to be fully understood.

Note: For much fuller explanations of the way ICT (information and communication technology) texts work, see two further books in this series: *The Language of ICT* by Tim Shortis and *The Language of Websites* by Mark Boardman.

PRODUCTION/RECEPTION

The meanings that are created within texts depend upon contextual factors at the point of production and reception, and the interface between these factors alters over time. Businesses in particular are aware of the need to change the attitudes of their potential customers and/or reflect what they see as changing attitudes in their customers. So, for example, the petrol company BP, at no doubt considerable cost, changed the visual representation of their name by going from capital letters to lower case – from BP to bp. This apparently small change will have been seen by the company as a vital step in influencing the way they are perceived. Use of lower-case letters, where traditionally upper-case have been used, was popular in the 1960s and now seems to be having a revival in the early 2000s. Meanwhile print texts are increasingly reflecting Internet language by being less linear in what they expect from a reader, and more bite-sized in the way they present information.

Activity

Research the ways children's encyclopedias have altered in the way they present information. It should be relatively easy to find copies of encyclopedias from the earlier part of the twentieth century as well as modern examples. You could extend your research by looking at entries which also highlight changes in social and political attitudes.

(Note: there is no commentary for this activity.)

VERBAL/VISUAL

Many contemporary texts have a creative interplay between the verbal and the visual. Text 17: Leeds and Holbeck Advertisement formed the back cover of an an information leaflet/application form for a credit card with the Leeds and Holbeck Building Society. It uses a mixture of visual and verbal techniques to achieve its purpose of encouraging prospective clients to apply for a credit card. Although it was printed in colour, many of its techniques can be analysed in this black and white reproduction.

Activity

◉   What well-known visual signs are used in the central part of Text 17: Leeds and Holbeck Advertisement, and how are they verbally 'cued'? In what ways is the well-known sign system extended beyond its usual set of signs?

◉   How is the writing at the top and bottom of the text graphologically varied?

Text 17: Leeds and Holbeck Advertisement

Commentary

The main semiotic system which is being played with here concerns the cleaning symbols which appear inside clothes. The basic symbols are as follows:

wash   bleach   tumble dry   press or iron   dry clean   do not

(In Britain the dry cleaning sign sometimes includes a P which stands for 'Professional', which suggests you should not try to dry clean the garment yourself, and/or 'Perchloroethylene', a cleaning chemical.)

You will notice here that some of the signs are iconic, in that they visually suggest what they signify in some way – 'wash', 'iron' and possibly 'tumble dry' come into that category. Others though are symbolic in that there is no visual correlation between sign and meaning – 'bleach' and 'dry clean' come into this category. The sign for 'do not' shows yet again the symbolic function of the 'x' sign.

The use of cleaning signs in this text is cued initially by the use of the word 'care' which is also highlighted – the idea of taking care of clothes and taking care of money is simultaneously implied. For the text to work with the reader, the reader needs to understand that a semiotic system they are already aware of is being used creatively to suggest a fresh set of meanings. In other words this text relies on intertextuality for much of its effect.

Some of the signs, such as the iron, the dry cleaning P and the tumble drier, are actual signs used in clothing, but with different meanings; because the comparison is a complex one, though, the important meanings (i.e. those to do with the credit card) are written underneath. The whole point of the signs, of course, is that on clothes labels they do not require words.

Other signs have elements of the original semiotic field, but subtly change them such as the crossed out pound and the 24 hour service. A further set of signs, such as the envelope and the mouse, do not appear in the original system, but they work here because they are made to look like the others, which we as readers have identified and are prepared to go along with. Notice that the made-up signs appear on the right hand side of each column. Because we read from left to right, we are 'programmed' by the earlier signs to accept these extra ones as part of the overall effect.

At the top of the text there is an italicised font which gives various information and the slogan 'It couldn't be simpler!!'. The two exclamation marks are designed to give double emphasis, as though the text is being spoken at this point. At the bottom are various features typical of a commercial text. There is a company logo, which uses different fonts and a box, and a company slogan beneath it, emphasising the word 'pays' which has a double meaning. In print of diminishing size, there is then a website address, which repeats the address given at the top, details about the bank underwriting the card and a code which probably identifies this leaflet.

The line which identifies the issuing bank is clearly seen as unimportant to readers of this text, compared to aspects of the credit card itself. To a different audience, though, such as workers in the banking sector, this would be a highly important piece of information.

If we take this text as in some ways typical of how advertising texts work in the twenty-first century, we can see the following visual and graphological points:

- different fonts are used to do different jobs in texts;

- different font sizes are used to rank ideas in order of priority;

- companies have various logos and slogans by which they can be readily identified;

- creative intertextual play is used to advertise the product;

- wordplay is signalled by highlighting key terms;

- an already known semiotic system is used and adapted.

Activity

Following the work you have just done on Text 17: Leeds and Holbeck Advertisement, now look at a text which first appeared in 1907. Make notes on the following question, and then where possible, compare your ideas with those of others.

- Bearing in mind contextual factors, how do visual elements and verbal elements of the text combine to make its meanings?

(Note: there is a commentary on this activity on p. 105.)

Text 18: Holiday Advertisement

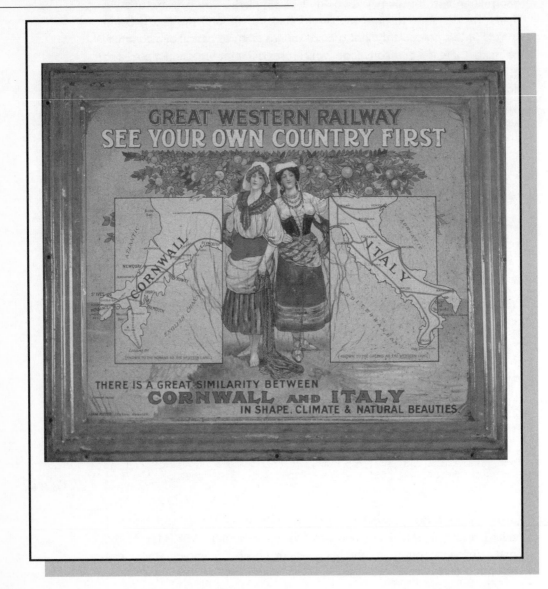

1   In the light of work done in this unit, write a commentary on Text 19: Nightmare/Nice Guy Postcard, which was a free postcard distributed in various outlets in Newcastle upon Tyne. This could be extended further to a research project based upon the genre of the free postcard.

Text 19: Nightmare/Nice Guy Postcard

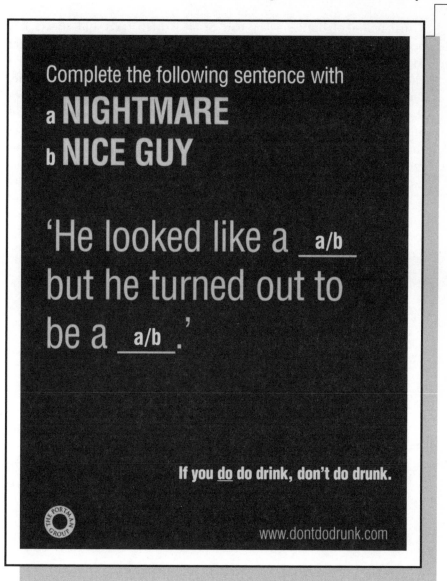

Complete the following sentence with
a **NIGHTMARE**
b **NICE GUY**

'He looked like a _a/b_ but he turned out to be a _a/b_.'

If you <u>do</u> do drink, don't do drunk.

www.dontdodrunk.com

2   This unit has stressed that some texts are becoming increasingly multi-modal. Reflect upon the texts that you produce as your writing repertoire. To what extent are they visual as well as verbal? To what extent are you allowed to be non-linear and bite-sized within academic contexts?

SUMMARY

Visual representation is a key part of all written texts and always has been. It is part of the system of meanings in a text rather than additional to them. Visual representation works through a series of cultural references and semiotic conventions, which can of course change over time. The signified meanings in texts are likely to involve attitudes and values that may no longer be commonly held. This means that when we read older texts, we will read them differently from people who read them at the time when they were first produced. Modern technology has led to multimodality being an increasing feature of texts, and visual representation has tended to become more symbolic and playful over time.

Unit five

Attitudes to language change

It is important to recognise at the start of this unit that all of us express attitudes towards the language used by other people. So, for example, we like to hear certain regional accents and dislike others, or there is often a current vogue word we 'cannot stand' but quite possibly start using ourselves, or there are taboo words which we believe should not be used in certain contexts and so on. All of us, to some extent, have attitudes towards language.

PUBLIC DEBATE

This vast reservoir of attitudes is sometimes channelled into a more public debate. A chance remark on a national radio station on 14 February 2003, that 'Valentines Day' was no longer being written with an apostrophe (Valentine's Day) led to a huge number of phone calls from the public and a growing debate about whether the English language was going to the dogs. In this debate the chair of the Apostrophe Protection Society (see p. 77) said that his life was full enough protecting the apostrophe and that he could not possibly take on any more causes.

Meanwhile newspapers, magazines and all sorts of other print media regularly print stories which express attitudes towards the way language is used 'incorrectly'. Language use, it seems, is a topic which will always get a response from the public, and frequently this use involves not so much language being used wrongly but language changing.

Activity

As a starting point for this topic, complete the following:

1   Make a list of the aspects of spoken language that you were corrected on as a child – and maybe are still being corrected on by parents/carers. You could take this further and as a piece of research collect data on what various parents/carers/teachers think should be corrected in children's spoken language.

2   Question a range of people about their attitudes to language use. This will almost certainly involve asking them what they dislike – positive views about language use are rarely heard outside discussions of literature.

3   Try to categorise the data you have collected in response to the above tasks. For example one category might be about right/wrong and another about pleasant/ugly.

Commentary

Donald Mackinnon (1996), categorises the attitudes people may have to language use. His main categories are:

◎   we may see language as *correct* or *incorrect*;

◎   we may judge some language examples to be *pleasant*, others *ugly*;

◎   we may judge some language examples to be *socially acceptable* and some *socially unacceptable*;

◎   we may judge some language examples to be *morally acceptable* and some *morally unacceptable*;

◎   we may find some language examples *appropriate in their context* and others *inappropriate in their context;*

◎   we may find some language examples *useful* to us or *useless.*

You can check your own data to find out how many categories you found evidence for.

....

TABOO

Part of the social and moral acceptability mentioned above involves taboo language. The main areas of human activity which are tradition-ally seen to have linguistic taboos are sex, death, bodily functions and religion. It is sex, bodily functions and religion which also provide much of the vocabulary that make up swearing. Harvey and Shalom (1997) note that a problem area in language is often indicated by the fact that there are many alternative variations of a concept which lacks a single unmarked form. (Unmarked here means a term which is 'neutral'.) They quote a range of categories which refer to sexual intercourse. These include:

◎   the technical (sexual intercourse, fornication, carnal knowledge);

◎   the mild and inoffensive or **euphemistic** ('go to bed with', 'sleep with', 'have sex with');

◎   the crude and vulgar or **dysphemistic** ('fuck', 'shag', 'screw', 'shaft', 'bonk').

It is the third category, the dysphemistic, which most would see as problematic, at least in some contexts. The list above should already have alerted you, though, to how important context is in the use of such terms, and that their usage is subject to change. Newspapers will use 'bonk' but not 'fuck', even though they have been placed in the same category above. When the play *Shopping and Fucking* by Mark Ravenhill was first staged, theatres faced the dilemma, intentional surely on the part of the author, as to whether they would advertise the full title of the play or use the traditional asterisk method to partially blank out the offending word. The solution of at least some, to show the full word, would suggest that the word 'fucking' is now less taboo than it once was.

73

On the other hand the Swedish Film *Fucking Amal* (Amal is a town in Sweden) became *Show me Love* when distributed in Britain. The clothing chain French Connection with its FCUK logo has produced an ever increasing range of logos and slogans which play with the near similarity of fcuk and fuck – the very fact that they are doing this, and that people wear the T-shirts, would suggest that the word still carries the power to shock, but without the absolute taboo of earlier times.

It must also be stressed though that there is a paradox around the idea of breaking a taboo. To use a taboo word in order to offend both breaks the taboo and at the same time reinforces it. Thus, some people say that overuse of taboo words in unnecessary contexts will gradually diminish their power to shock and so deprive us of useful language items: taboo terms support us in the occasional need to shock, to register outrage, or to express disappointment or pain.

As with all language change, attitudes towards taboos change not only over time but according to context. Most people would accept that language around sex and death is less euphemistic than it was fifty years ago, but there are also variations within current use. Depending upon your age, sex, social class etc. your use of taboo language will vary. Harvey and Shalom (1997) also note that taboo language can have a very different function in private from that which it has in public. So, for example, sexual partners may well 'play' with all sorts of taboo language as part of their relationship together.

Activity

Using the three categories above, technical, euphemistic and dysphemistic, make lists of words which refer to female and male genitalia. Which words would you use with children to talk about and name their private parts? Which words would you use in sex education classes at school?

(Note: there is no commentary for this activity.)

CHANGE OR DIFFERENCE?

Often the attitudes that people have towards language use is not so much about language change as about language variety. Take for example some of the controversies around the way words are pronounced.

Read aloud the following words, trying to repeat how you say them 'naturally' when you are not thinking about them:

adult

ate

controversy

data

dilemma

secretary

trait

Each of these can in fact be pronounced in at least two distinct ways – many more if regional accents are taken into account. Robert Burchfield (1981), gives advice to 'announcers and presenters on the BBC networks' on pronunciation and other matters. He says the following is the way the words above should be pronounced:

adult	–	stress on first syllable;
ate	–	rhymes with 'bet' not with 'bait';
controversy	–	stress on first syllable;
data	–	first syllable as in 'rate';
dilemma	–	first syllable with short I, not as in 'tie';
secretary	–	(sec-re-tree) not (sec-e-tree);
trait	–	final t is silent.

In making these judgements, he is also acknowledging that there are in fact other ways of saying the words, that he is choosing one variant over another. He prefaces his judgements by writing: 'it is assumed that the speaker uses Received Standard English in its 1980s form. The form of speech recommended is that of a person born and brought up in one of the Home Counties and educated at one of the established southern universities.' Here he is giving preference to a complete social package, including region, education and, by implication, social class. In many areas of language use, therefore, although people think they are objecting to language being in some way changed, they are actually objecting to one social dialect as against another.

Similarly, the endless debate about the split infinitive in English (endless in that it has been going on for well over a hundred years) is not really about language change as such. The *New Oxford Dictionary of English* in 1998 suggested that:

> It is still widely held that splitting infinitives is wrong. The dislike of split infinitives is long-standing but is not well founded, being based on an analogy with Latin . . . But English is not the same as Latin. In particular the placing of an adverb in English is extremely important in giving the appropriate emphasis . . . 'You have to really watch him' conveys a different emphasis from 'you really have to watch him'.

This was greeted by howls of outrage in some national newspapers. Writing in the *Daily Telegraph* (14 August 1998) Tom Utley denied that allowing split infinitives is broadly accepted:

> Broadly accepted by whom? Not I suspect by people who think and care enough about the language to know what a split infinitive is . . . there are very good reasons of taste, style and good manners for not splitting infinitives.

Here then we have a defence of one variant of grammatical usage on grounds that are essentially nothing to do with language – references to 'caring' about language, 'taste' and 'good manners' are to do with social values rather than language use and language change. Language 'rules' are being invented in order to endorse a social ideology. Texts from the last four hundred years show that the infinitive has, in fact, often been split in English, so 'to boldly go' is not, as such, an example of recent language change. It suits an essentially conservative ideology, though, to latch on to such grammatical 'errors' and to use them as examples of declining standards in modern life.

1   Take a walk down a local shopping street and make a list of the various
    shop signs. What do you notice about such things as: fonts used, apos-
    trophes used or not, other punctuation, upper/lower case? Is it possible
    to say such signs are wrong?

    This could also form the data for a wider investigation

2   The stated aim of the Apostrophe Protection Society is:

    > preserving the correct use of this currently much abused
    > punctuation mark in all forms of text written in the English
    > language.
    >
    > > (see website: www.apostrophe.fsnet.co.uk)

    The 'Language Live Home for Abused Apostrophes', on the other hand,
    would appear to take a more relaxed view of how apostrophes are
    used. It offers:

    > a haven for little punctuation marks cruelly misused by
    > greengrocers and other uncaring notice writers.
    >
    > > (see website: www.nuff.ox.ac.uk/Users/
    > > Martin/APOST/Apostrop.htm)

    Access both websites and consider the attitudes to language change
    that they seem to represent.

(Note: there is no commentary for this activity.)

PRESCRIPTION/DESCRIPTION

So far this unit has referred to aspects of taboo, pronunciation, punctuation and grammar, and some of the controversies that surround these.
As Jean Aitchison noted in her BBC Reith Lecture entitled 'Is our
language in decay?':

> All languages have their 'rules' in the sense of recurring subcon-
> scious patterns. In English we place the verb inside the sentence,
> and say 'The spider caught the fly' ... but real rules need to be
> distinguished from artificially imposed ones. For example ... an old

and illogical belief that logic should govern language has led in English to a ban on the double negative.

Aitchison argues against what is sometimes called a **prescriptive** view of language. A prescriptive view of language identifies a vast network of rules and then checks English usage against these rules, often, in the process, using an essentially written model of English to assess the quality of spoken English. Prescriptive approaches to language, by definition, involve those who know the 'rules' standing in judgement over those who apparently do not. Contrary to popular belief, most communication does work, and if it doesn't the communicators do something about it. When someone says 'I don't know nothing about it', the meaning is perfectly clear, even though the double negative has been used. Indeed it could be argued that the denial in the statement above is all the stronger for being doubled.

So, many of the complaints by the prescriptive camp are not about failure to communicate, but about failure to communicate in a certain way. Think for example of the very common complaint that young people are lazy in their speech and cannot be understood. It may well be that young people want to convey some attitude in what they say, but they do communicate and they are not lazy – the only lazy speech, as Jean Aitchison has pointed out, is when you are drunk and lose full control of your mouth and tongue.

One organisation which advocates a prescriptive approach to language is the Queen's English Society, whose very name conjures up a value judgement about what constitutes 'good' or 'correct' English. As part of its overall rationale the society says:

> The Society aims to defend the precision, subtlety and marvellous richness of our language against debasement, ambiguity and other forms of misuse ... Although it accepts that there is always a natural development of any language, the Society deplores those changes which are the result of ignorance and which become established because of indifference.
>
> (www.author.co.uk/qes/)

The use of the word 'established' in the above quotation, though, does suggest that attempts to halt certain changes do not and cannot work. **Descriptive** approaches to language, therefore, analyse and comment on how language is used, but without any attempt to pass value judgements on such changes.

The following sentences all contain examples of 'incorrect' English, according to the prescriptive model. Can you say what is 'wrong' in each example and would you use such English yourself? Assume that all of these are spoken examples, except number 4.

1   Hopefully the bus will come soon.

2   A lecturer and us are going to the theatre.

3   He did it all off his own back.

4   They were alright after the accident.

5   I was really bored and disinterested in that lecture.

6   They will try and get here today.

(Note: there is a commentary on this activity on p. 106.)

PLAIN ENGLISH

One organisation which makes value judgements on the way English is used, but from a very different standpoint to the Queen's English Society, is the Plain English Campaign. This organisation is not concerned with 'good' or 'correct' English as such, but with English that communicates effectively with ordinary people, and so avoids what is sometimes called **gobbledygook**. Gobbledygook can be defined as language which is unnecessarily difficult to understand: this can be because it is very dense in its structures, or because it uses terminology that is not generally accessible. This is relevant to a book on language change because the Plain English Campaign is seeking to intervene in some of the language practices that it sees as essentially undemocratic. Here, then, we have language change approached from a perspective of language reform.

On its website, www.plainenglish.co.uk, it makes the following statements:

What is plain English?

We define plain English as something that the intended audience can read, understand and act upon the first time they read it. Plain English takes into account design and layout as well as language.

Where should plain English be used?

Plain English is needed in all kinds of public information, such as forms, leaflets, agreements and contracts. The golden rule is that plain English should be used in any information that ordinary people rely on when they make decisions.

What's wrong with gobbledygook?

We can't put it better than a nurse who wrote to us about a baffling memo. She said that 'receiving information in this form makes us feel hoodwinked, inferior, definitely frustrated and angry, and it causes a divide between us and the writer.'

Both the Queen's English Society and the Plain English Campaign see themselves as campaigning on aspects of English usage. Whereas the former seems to be concerned with things such as the beauty and rules of language, the latter is campaigning for language to be clear and accessible in its meanings.

The following are 'before' and 'after' examples taken from the Plain English Campaign's website. 'Before' refers to the original text, and 'after' the new version from the Plain English Campaign.

Before

If there are any points on which you require explanation or further particulars we shall be glad to furnish such additional details as may be required by telephone.

After

If you have any questions, please ring.

Before

Your enquiry about the use of the entrance area at the library for the purpose of displaying posters and leaflets about Welfare and Supplementary Benefit rights, gives rise to the question of the provenance and authoritativeness of the material to be displayed. Posters and leaflets issued by the Central Office of Information, the Department of Health and Social Security and other authoritative bodies are usually displayed in libraries, but items of a disputatious or polemic kind, whilst not necessarily excluded, are considered individually.

After

Thank you for your letter asking permission to put up posters in the entrance area of the library. Before we can give you an answer we will need to see a copy of the posters to make sure they won't offend anyone.

What, then, is the difference between the approaches to language as exemplified by the Queen's English Society and the Plain English Campaign? In some ways their names say it all. The former represents a view of language that is about knowledge possessed by some and not others, whereas the latter is about general access to meaning in public texts. In other words one is autocratic and one democratic.

POLITICAL CORRECTNESS

Political correctness is a label used to refer to social practices as well as the language used to describe such practices. So, for example, in a series entitled 'Council Killjoys', the *Sun* (22 August 2002) began an article 'Barmy bureaucrats banned a Punch and Judy show for promoting domestic violence'. The *Daily Express* (13 December 2002) in an article subtitled 'Kids told Christ is outdated', began 'Teachers were accused of peddling politically correct nonsense yesterday after telling pupils to stop using the Christian calendar'.

If looked at closely, both articles show some common features of the way political correctness is commonly presented:

> Barmy bureaucrats banned a Punch and Judy show for promoting domestic violence.

> Teachers were accused of peddling politically correct nonsense yesterday after telling pupils to stop using the Christian calendar.

Consider, for example, the following:

◎ one group of people is accused by another;

◎ the accusers are often not specified;

◎ the accusation involves allegations of stupidity – 'barmy', 'nonsense';

◎ there is a serious topic (e.g. domestic violence, religious tolerance) but a sense that political correctness goes too far.

Studying the notion of 'political correctness' is relevant to many areas of language study, because language is a form of behaviour. It is relevant in a book on language change because whereas many examples of change take place over time, and are essentially unconscious in their use, change through so-called political correctness involves a conscious process, whereby we are making known choices in the language we use, and reflecting on such uses. In Donald Mackinnon's categories of attitudes referred to earlier, one is of relevance to the notion of political correctness. This is that we may judge some examples of language use to be *morally acceptable* and some *morally unacceptable*. The problem with ideas around political correctness, though, is that it is rarely as clear-cut as whether a term is morally unacceptable or not, and it is rare to find complete agreement on what terms should be used. It also needs to be pointed out here that the term itself is not the only language issue; how the term is used, by whom to whom and in what context must also be examined.

In a companion book in this series, *Language and Gender*, Goddard and Patterson (2000) explore in detail aspects of this topic, with particular regard to the history of the term itself, and how it relates to aspects of gender. It is well worth reading Unit four of their book, in addition to what follows below.

While sounding as though it is a positive term, because of the word 'correct', the phrase 'politically correct' is in fact nowadays largely used negatively – as a criticism of language use. It is also important to stress at this point that it is not possible to use the phrase 'politically correct' neutrally. If you say something is politically correct, then you yourself are making a political judgement on the attitudes shown by others. Those who criticise modern English usage are often the very same people who object most to political correctness in language; those who believe current usage in general needs reform are therefore at the same time saying that language should not be reformed when it comes to certain sensitive social issues.

Notions of political correctness are concerned with aspects of language and power; where language use is criticised for being politically correct, such use is to do with social groups who are in some way seen to be in a minority and disadvantaged. So, for example, when in September 2000 the Greater Manchester Police Force issued a document called *The Power of Language: A Practical Guide to the Use of Language* it included sections on the following: 'Age and Language', 'Disability and Language', 'Gender and Language', 'Race, Ethnicity and Language', 'Religion and Language' and 'Sexual Orientation and Language'. In its preface, the document said the following:

> Greater Manchester Police is a professional organisation and it is essential that we take a lead in using language that does not exclude members of the community . . . we are aware that there are varying views in the police service about the importance of language as an equality issue. The important point is to be sensitive to the issues, and the possible offence language can cause.

In saying that language can cause offence, it is implied here that the hurt is caused to the hearer/reader of the offensive language. 'Offensive' language, though, in addition to causing hurt to the hearer/ reader can also expose the intentions and prejudices of the speaker/ writer.

83

Activity

The first section in the Manchester Police document referred to above is entitled 'Age and Language'. It includes the following:

Text 20: Manchester Police: Age and Language

Age and neutral terminology

We clearly should not make assumptions about the value of people based upon their age. It is better to use neutral terms such as elderly or older when referring to people. For example:

- Services for elderly people
- Elderly relatives
- Older workers

Unacceptable terminology

'Old' in this society carries connotations of being worn out and of little further use. It is even used as a term of abuse. For example the following terms may offend some people:

- Old fool
- Old codger
- Old dear
- Old biddy

Consider the following questions:

1   How do you respond to the advice above? Should the police use language in a way that requires such suggestions?

2   Does the word 'old' always carry negative **connotations**?

3   In a section on 'Age', there is no reference to the way young people are addressed. Should there be? If so what terms would be unacceptable?

(Note: there is no commentary for this activity.)

The Manchester Police document (which can be found on www.gmp. police.uk) has eighteen pages of text and includes only one reference to political correctness. It says:

> The label 'politically correct' is often used as an excuse, a criticism or an accusation by people unwilling or unable to take responsibility for their actions.

When the document became public and was reported in the press, however, reports focused on political correctness as being at the heart of the issue. A typical headline was:

> STRICTLY PC: THE POLICE GUIDE TO BAD LANGUAGE
> (*Metro* 21 September 2000)

and in a number of reports a 'senior officer with more than twenty years' experience' was quoted as saying:

> This document is a waste of time. Police have enough on their plates these days without adding to the problems. This document makes out that we are all idiots who need to be told how to address people. We are human beings who are trained to deal with tricky situations, this report makes a mockery of that. We're scared to open our mouths in case we offend anybody.

Activity

1   Comment on the way the headline quoted above represents this issue.

2   Comment on the attitude to language shown in the quotation above.

Commentary

The headline makes an obvious play on the fact that PC can mean two things: it can stand for police constable or for political correctness. In saying that this is a guide to 'bad language' it deliberately focuses on a negative, whereas in fact it could be argued that the police are being urged to use 'good' language. This negative mood is endorsed by the quotation from the unnamed senior officer. His seniority and experience are used to support his negative views on the document. In essence he (we must assume it is a 'he') is saying that there are better things to do than worry about language, that 'tricky situations' are not helped by having to think about what you say. It could be argued, though, that these tricky situations could have been made tricky *because* of the language used – in other words language is part of the problem not an addition to it.

SELF-LABELS

Text 20: Manchester Police: Age and Language, shown earlier in this unit, is taken from a document which looks at the way one group, the police, should address another less powerful group, the old. This suggests that much of the debate over political correctness is about naming 'others', but as part of the debate we need to consider how such people label themselves. Writing in the *Independent* (26 November 2002), Philip Hensher said:

> To take away the right of people to their own name, to how they choose to refer to themselves, is an act of subjugation and disapproval. To ask people what they want to call themselves, and then use that name is, on the other hand, an act of ordinary respect ... Paedophiles probably don't refer to themselves as paedophiles, but we stick to our name and not theirs, because we disapprove of the preference, and generally don't accept that they have a right to self-determination ... Whether you ask someone what they want to be called, or whether you decide on their behalf what they ought to be called, is a gauge of the respect that society is prepared to offer its constituent groups.

Hensher goes on to point out that the situation is made more complex by the fact that people in a group can call each other names that outsiders cannot. Discussing the difficulty how gay men should describe themselves he says:

> there was a brave attempt to reclaim 'queer' and turn it into a rallying call, but it has a slightly period feel now. Moreover, it is one of those words, like 'poof', that we cheerfully use to each other, but that we would certainly not want anyone else to use.

A further problem with how groups are labelled is that they tend to be seen as homogenous groups – because you are gay, you are 'placed' with other gay people, when there are many ways in which you are different, such as your age, regional background etc.

Extension

So far the account of attitudes held towards language change have concentrated on the way British users of English reflect upon their language. There is, though, a much bigger picture which can be looked at when considering attitudes to language change, a picture which takes into account the fact that English is a 'world language'. Broadly speaking attitudes to English as a world language can be subdivided as follows:

- there are attitudes to the fact that English is used rather than other languages;

- and there are attitudes to the fact that English itself is being changed by having an international dimension.

Possible areas of research include:

- English as a **lingua franca** in such **restricted languages** as 'airspeak' and 'seaspeak';

- English lexical items in other languages such as 'franglais' in French;

- attempts to make English into an international language through strategies such as BASIC;

- differences between American and British English and attitudes to such differences;

- other Standard Englishes such as Scottish, Australian etc.;

- resistance to the domination of English for example in Wales;

- **pidgin** and **creole** variations of Standard English;

- **code-switching** among and across ethnic groups.

SUMMARY

This unit has explored various attitudes to language and in particular language change. It has referred to taboo language, prescription and description, various campaigns on language, and political correctness. Public discourses about language have a tendency towards negativity, a criticism of the way language is used by some people and how such language is in some ways 'wrong'. In our own more private usage, though, we are happily resistant to such criticism and go on being inventive and playful.

Internal aspects of change

At the beginning of this book it was noted that it is possible to explore ideas about language change by looking at the *internal* history of a language and the *external* history of a language. Throughout this book so far the focus has been on the way external factors have influenced and are influencing language change. This final unit, however, will briefly summarise some of the more technical areas which have traditionally been at the heart of work on language change. In looking at such internal areas, though, it is important to stress again that language change always has a context and that language changes because of all the social, political and technological issues which affect the way language is used to communicate.

Although it has looked at context as a driving force behind language change, this book has been 'traditional' in two important ways. The first is that it has tended to focus on written texts, with relatively little reference to spontaneous face-to-face unmediated talk. The second is that it has used Standard English as its main point of reference, rather than other regional and/or social dialects. It should be remembered, though, that all aspects of language change over time, and that it would be just as possible to chart aspects of change within spoken discourse and within regional dialects.

LEXICAL CHANGE

At 'lexical' or word level it is possible to comment on a number of aspects of language change. These usually involve the introduction of 'new' lexical items into the language – although words also fall out of use, they are, by definition, rarely noticed to be doing so.

One way in which new words enter the language is by **borrowing** from another language. (Reversing the financial metaphor, such words are also known as **loan words** – but in both cases there is no sense that the original language is ever paid back.) English is a frequent borrower of words, with nouns and adjectives being the most frequent categories, adverbs and pronouns the least. Often a word has an anglicised spelling based upon how the word was heard. So, for example, from Arabic we have 'alcohol', 'alcove', 'assassin', from Hindi 'bungalow', 'dungaree', 'shampoo'. When first arriving into the language they are often written in inverted commas, or by using italics. As they become more subsumed into the language, though, such markers disappear.

A large number of borrowed lexical items refer to eating and drinking, with the words in their original language carrying an extra sense of being exotic. In Britain in particular French food (or cuisine) has traditionally been seen as sophisticated. The connotations around food terminology are subtle and fast changing. So, for example, the word 'café' (often pronounced in an English way as 'caff') was often quite low status but has now moved up-market again if pronounced in the French way. 'Brasserie' and 'bistro' are other French words with a specific set of connotations when used in British English.

The use of **affixes** is a highly productive source of lexical development and invention. **Suffixes** tend to change the class of a word and can at the same time expand upon its range of meaning. So the noun 'profession', which usually refers to certain types of occupation, gives the adjective 'professional' with its much wider range of meanings. (Consider for example the use of 'professional foul' in sport.) **Prefixes** are usually much more obviously tied to meaning. So, for example, the prefix 'hyper' (from the Greek for 'over'/'beyond') can be added to many nouns to give a sense of bigness or extensiveness ('hypermarket', 'hypertext', 'hyper-inflation') and can even stand alone as with 'hyper', a short form of 'hyperactive'. 'Mega', also suggesting vastness, can be added to many nouns and also for a while existed as a fashionable 'word' in its own right.

Back-formation involves losing rather than adding an element to a word, so the verb 'to edit' comes from 'editor' and 'to commentate' from 'commentator'. **Clipping** is another form of abbreviation, examples being 'veg', 'fan', 'deli'. **Compounding** adds two words together as in 'body-blow', 'jet set', with such compounds sometimes using a hyphen to show that two words have been put together. **Blending** adds elements of two words together as in 'brunch', 'electrocute'.

Acronyms and **initialisms** are even more extreme forms of abbreviation. Acronyms are 'words' made out of the initial letters of a phrase, such as 'SATS'. Sometimes the name of the organisation is deliberately arranged so that it can have a creative acronym, as in 'ASH', which stands for Action on Smoking and Health. The **tautology** in the name of the epidemic 'SARS', Severe Acute Respiratory Syndrome, is presumably there to avoid an otherwise unfortunate acronym; and the teachers' organisation 'NUT' uses an initialism even though its name could be an acronym – but not a very flattering one.

In contrast to abbreviations, **noun phrases**, although not strictly single words, can be seen as lexical units. So, for example, in the sentence 'The temperamental left-sided footballer with classical good looks scored on his debut', the core noun 'footballer' is pre-modified with 'temperamental left-sided' and post-modified with 'with classical good looks'.

Many of the methods described above are used by commercial organisations when naming companies and products. So, for example, the florist 'FLOWERSTALK' uses a blend of two words to create a cleverly ambiguous pair of meanings.

Activity

Look again at Text 4: Bank of Scotland Investment Service Recruitment which appears earlier in this book (p. 13). What examples of 'new' lexical items can be found here?

(Note: there is a commentary on this activity on p. 106.)

SPELLING

Although the English written alphabet has twenty-six letters, these letters and their combinations represent something like forty-four basic sounds. George Bernard Shaw famously highlighted what he saw as the eccentricity of English spelling by spelling the word 'fish' as 'ghoti': 'gh' from 'tough'; 'o' from 'women'; and 'ti' from 'fruition'. Shaw was one of a number of people who have tried over the years to rationalise spelling by deliberate change. The ITA (Initial Teaching Alphabet) was popular in schools in the 1960s and 1970s as an aid to early literacy. Although spelling is as arbitrary as any other aspect of language, any attempt to change spelling meets fierce opposition. There are many more aspects to writing than spelling 'correctly', yet for many people 'being able to spell' is the most important sign of whether someone is literate.

Spelling has undergone steady change over time, although the standardisation of spelling through dictionaries has obviously slowed this process. In Britain there is particular disdain for what are seen as American spellings, such as 'flavor', 'theater', 'fulfill'. These though are attitudes to the culture of the language users rather than being logical objections. The use of spell-checkers on computers has added another layer of controversial 'authority' and the dominance of Microsoft often reinforces American patterns. As was seen in Unit three, new modes of communication such as texting have led to alternative ways of spelling, and subsequent cries of horror about declining standards. Meanwhile commercial organisations in particular 'play' with spelling to create various effects: listings in the Tyneside telephone directory include: 'Xpress Ironing', 'Xpertise Training', 'Xsite Architecture', 'Xtreme Talent' and 'Xyst Marketing Agency'.

The printing process, which has had a huge influence on the standardisation of spelling, itself has a history of change. So, for example, the similarity between the way 's' and 'f' were printed in the sixteenth and seventeenth century allowed poets like Shakespeare and Donne to make rude jokes, as in 'where the bee sucks there suck I'.

Activity

Comment on the spelling to be found in the following two texts:

◎   Text 15: Shakespeare Dedication (Unit four, p. 58)

◎   Text 13: Emails (Unit three, p. 47)

(Note: there is a commentary on this activity on p. 106.)

PUNCTUATION

Punctuation involves a set of marks which order texts and clarify mean-ings, principally by separating or linking (and also by using parentheses and asides). Punctuation also helps to suggest how a text should sound if read aloud. In the eighteenth and nineteenth century writers tended to punctuate heavily, partly because their syntax was often more complex. Nowadays punctuation is less heavily used in formal texts, but in informal use some marks are used heavily to suggest a certain emotional impact. So a question followed by '???' could be seen as particularly enigmatic, and a string of exclamation marks suggests a particularly significant point!!

Inevitably there are attitudes to punctuation use which overlaps with spelling. Some lament the loss of the hyphen in compound words such as *coordinate, worldwide* (which this computer spell-checker does not allow), others ridicule the added apostrophe that is often seen in certain plurals such as *tomato's* and *CD's*.

Activity

Comment on the punctuation in the following texts:

◎　Text 9: The Lord of Devonshire His Pudding (Unit two, p. 30)

◎　Text 13: Emails (Unit three, p. 47)

(Note: there is a commentary on this activity on p. 107.)

GRAMMAR

A detailed history of English would focus on grammatical changes over hundreds of years. One of the most significant overall changes under-gone in the English language is that it has lost most of its **inflections**; some give this as a reason why English is supposedly easy to learn as a non-native speaker. Inflections do occur on verbs by adding suffixes suggesting such things as tense (walk, walks, walking), on nouns for plurality and possession (mothers, mother's) and on some adjectives for comparison (wide, wider, widest).

Relatively speaking grammar has changed very little in recent times, but where there is alternative usage, strong attitudes are often held. One area of particular concern to some is in the so-called misuse of **irregular verbs**. Whereas Standard English has for example, 'saw' or 'did', some regional dialects have 'seen' or 'done'. Giving media access to people with regional dialects, especially in such areas as sports commentary, has given a more public airing to such dialect usage in speech.

MEANING AND ETYMOLOGY

Changes in meaning can be looked at via **denotative** meanings and connotative meanings. The word 'nice' which now means 'pleasant' or 'agreeable' originally meant 'ignorant', coming from the Latin *nescire* meaning 'not know'. Gradually the word moved through 'coy' to 'particular/distinct', a meaning which it can still have, and then on to its most usual present meaning. Context, though, is all, and it is possible to use the word 'nice' with quite negative connotations. If you describe your new love interest as 'nice', your friend might conclude that the relationship will not last. If you tell your friend that their new jacket is 'nice' they might well think that you don't like it that much. So, denotative meanings in dictionaries can be limited in their scope; a whole range of contextual factors can subtly affect what a word or phrase on any single occasion.

One area of meaning worth thinking about with regard to language change involves metaphor. Whereas literary metaphors tend to be obvious in the comparisons they make ('I wandered lonely as a cloud') there are many so-called dead metaphors where the original comparison is less obvious. Linguists such as Lakoff and Johnson (1980) and Andrew Goatly (1997) have shown how many 'dead' metaphors exist in English and how they can subtly affect the way we think about the world. When a blind student says 'I see' when solving a problem in class, they are referring to the mental act of understanding via the physical act of seeing – and nobody in the class notices that a blind student is talking about being able to see.

How meanings change, and the metaphorical origins of many meanings can be traced via the **etymology** of a word or phrase. Many reasonably sized dictionaries will give the etymology of a word, and there are also specialist etymological dictionaries.

Comment on the use of metaphor in the following texts:

◎ Text 8B: Republic of Ireland v Spain (2002) (Unit two, p. 24)

◎ Text 15: Shakespeare Dedication (Unit four, p. 58)

(Note: there is a commentary on this activity on p. 107.)

PRONUNCIATION

When Shakespeare puts the words 'death-mark'd love' and 'could remove' in a rhyme scheme at the beginning of *Romeo and Juliet*, this causes problems for modern readers and actors – there is no way that 'love' and 'remove' rhyme in modern Standard English. The fact that they are in a rhyme scheme as part of a sonnet is strong evidence that to Shakespeare these words would have rhymed. From close attention to such things as rhyme it is possible to have some idea of how Shakespeare's plays may have sounded to contemporary audiences. Recording equipment gives us much clearer evidence that as recently as the 1940s and 1950s actors such as Olivier and Gielgud sound very different from actors nowadays.

Pronunciation then, like everything else in language, changes over time, and because it involves the sounds of language, and so is very obvious, it leads to particularly strong attitudes. For some people in Britain the pronunciation of 'data' with a short first 'a' sound is like nails scraping on a blackboard. In Britain, there are often hostile attitudes to what is perceived to be American pronunciation. The so-called 'mid-Atlantic drawl' of some radio disc jockeys and television presenters has been much mocked, with a recent trend being to replace them with presenters who have a clearly obvious British regional accent. (Although the range of accents is not equally distributed – there are far more Irish and Geordie than Glaswegian or Brummie.) When a president or other public figure stresses the first syllable 'u' on 'United States' a whole host of attitudes can be released in British hearers.

A BBC guide to pronunciation in 1981 recommended that broadcasters should use the following:

adults   –   stress first syllable

aristocrat   –   stress on first syllable

95

comparable	–	stress on first syllable
controversy	–	stress on first syllable
decade	–	stress on first syllable
contribute	–	stress on second syllable
dispute	–	stress on second syllable
distribute	–	stress on second syllable
harass	–	stress on first syllable
research	–	stress on second syllable

Almost certainly, though, despite such instructions, the pronunciation of these words is subtly shifting.

It is not just individual words though that undergo change. Australian 'soaps' have been blamed (note that language change is rarely given credit!) for the upwards intonation that increasingly occurs at the end of an utterance, regardless of whether it is a question or not. Where pronunciation patterns are associated with young people in particular there are likely to be polarised attitudes; older people will deplore, younger people will find common identity.

Extension

Each of the sections above can provide useful starting points for further language investigation. The following are just some of the possibilities.

Lexical change

◎ *Commercial names*: it is easy to collect data on names for shops and products. If you can find a suitable niche to specialise in, it is possible to find various ways of categorising your material.

◎ *Borrowing*: one possible angle on language borrowing is to see how English is used in non-English-speaking countries. Possible data could include public signs, such as in department stores or shop names, and products such as clothing, shoes etc.

◎ Another possibility could involve looking at the way food is named and described, especially in contexts where food outlets and products are associated with a specific country or region. The naming and description of drinks is also a possibility.

◎ You could also survey the national and local press over a period of, say, one week and see what 'new' words are used, and the context that they are used in.

Spelling

◎ Access to data from other English-speaking countries, especially the US, could lead to the collection of some comparative data.

◎ Lists of 'problem' spellings can be compiled and data collected on whether people can spell these words.

◎ Spelling, and attitudes to it, can be explored by looking at the writing of young children, and how their teachers respond to it.

◎ Yellow Pages, and other directories of names, can help to provide data on the way commercial organisations use creative spelling.

Punctuation

◎ Electronic texts such as emails can be explored for the different uses of punctuation marks.

◎ The signs on shops and businesses offer some interesting data opportunities. Do they use apostrophes for short forms or possession (e.g. *Lloyd's Bank* but *Boots*), full stops, upper- or lower-case letters etc.?

◎ Street stalls and market stalls can be explored for use of what is sometimes called the 'greengrocer's apostrophe', i.e. an apostrophe added to a simple plural.

Grammar

Attitudes to non-standard grammatical forms – often called grammatical 'mistakes' – can be acquired via an attitudes survey or questionnaire. So, for example, you can discover if people are aware of the non-standard forms, and how strongly they object to their use by others. Areas you could cover include such things as past tenses of irregular verbs, pronoun/verb agreement, subject/object pronouns etc.

Meaning and etymology

◎ Although finding the etymology of words can be interesting on a personal level, copying out lists of etymologies will not make for a particularly interesting investigation. A better idea would be to find words, pairs of words and idioms where the current meaning seems to be shifting, and to survey people on what they think the meanings are. Examples to use might include uninterested/disinterested, flaunt/flout and the expressions 'it will all come out in the wash' and 'off your own bat/back'.

◎ If you are interested in metaphor, you could take a broad conceptual area such as 'learning = a journey of discovery' and trace the various uses of this metaphor in your school/college literature.

Pronunciation

For relatively amateur linguists, investigating pronunciation can be very difficult, because you may not have a knowledge of phonetic transcription, and you may not have the 'ear' for minor differences. Even asking people to pronounce words into a tape can be a problem as they will not be speaking naturally, without thinking about how they say things.

It is, though, possible to find out attitudes to pronunciation (and indeed other aspects of dialect) provided you have good access to examples which you can let people hear.

answers and commentaries

Unit one (Text 2), p. 7

Bob Morton is presented as having certain characteristics. He is intelligent, artistic, tough but not aggressive, proud of doing a good job. He also has what can be seen as social qualities: he speaks 'better' than the locals, he has a smart set of gloves, he is clean in his habits, he does what is expected of him without argument. Although he is seen by the young miners to be a 'snob', because we see things from his point of view we can understand that the narrative of the story is guiding us towards approval of Bob. He is not a snob, he is a hero. It is unlikely though that such qualities would be the hallmark of a hero in a contemporary story.

If Bob is seen as heroic, then the young miners are seen as narrow-minded and vindictive. Mining is seen as uncomfortable and dangerous, but essentially a job that can be done by someone like Bob. Describing the coal itself as black diamonds makes it sound rather romantic.

There is a range of terms here which depict males: the book itself is for 'boys', Bob is a 'Bevin boy', the other workers are 'pit lads' (possibly to denote regional dialect), the work is 'a man's job' and the one name that Bob cannot stand is 'The Pansy Pitboy'. In terms of a wider representation of masculinity, this is closely tied in with social class. Bob, the hero, is artistic yet tough, able to do a 'man's job' yet have a passion for drawing. In the end, though, he needs to prove that he is a man by being hard not soft, by fighting and winning.

One audience for this story is young boys who are likely to come from a similar background to Bob – southern English, educated, middle class, the sort of boys who were bought *The Monster Book for Boys* as a Christmas present. Another audience might be boys whose parents were aspirant enough to hope that their sons might belong to such a social background. It is unlikely, though, that such a story would be read by 'pit lads'. The story's audience is addressed via a vocabulary and syntax that sound rather formal to modern ears: the sentence 'He had stood a lot of twitting on account of them' is one good example of such formality, the phrase 'drawing was a passion with Bob' another. The worst abuse that Dick Haslam can come up with is to call Bob 'The Pansy Pitboy' and even that is not said directly to him.

Presenting the conflict here as existing between an enlightened outsider and narrow-minded pit boys glosses over what we know were the problems faced by the Bevin boys. The story becomes one of simple class conflict, with a middle-class hero and a working-class villain, rather than a criticism of the system itself. It is probably quite easy to come up with a typical ending for this story, because we know the genre within which it is working. In fact Bob refuses to fight with Dick Haslam and is therefore despised even more, but when there is an emergency Bob shows courage and saves the day. Then he does fight and beat Dick, after which the two 'walked off home together – the Kid-Glove Collier and Dick Haslam, his new pal!'. In other words, Bob has shown all the virtues of the ruling class, and in doing so won over the prejudiced member of the lower orders.

Obviously one purpose of this story was to entertain the boys who read it. In hindsight we can see that another much more powerful purpose of this story was to support an ideological view of life in England, a view that in many ways supported the status quo.

Unit two (Text 7), p. 21

Although it is presented as a block of text, with only a dash to suggest the reply, there is a clear question and answer format here. Cymon, presumably a pseudonym, presents a problem in the first person voice and then asks for advice. The advice, though, is not given to him directly, with the reader acting as an eavesdropper as we would expect nowadays. Instead the reply is about him in the third person.

There are many contextual aspects which give this text a period feel. Most of these involve notions of courtship and relationships between the sexes, presented by Cymon from a distinctly masculine perspective. This woman has done the unforgivable – been unfaithful to him. Much of the vocabulary used by Cymon in particular is therefore both formal sounding and melodramatic.

Because the request part of the text is so 'typically' Victorian, the reply comes as something of a surprise. Cymon is quite firmly put in his place and shown to be a man who needs to see some sense. Having first given some possible practical reasons for the woman's behaviour, the 'we' who speak the text advise him actually to go and talk to the woman. The reply, despite being couched in a formal way carries sentiments which would not be out of place in a similar column today – except perhaps for marriage being seen as the ultimate resolution of the problem.

This text, then, shows that we should be careful not to prejudge social attitudes and values, and that we should look carefully at both the text itself and contextual details which surround it. The fact that this text appeared in a women's magazine helps to explain the nature of the reply.

Unit two (Text 10), p. 31

◎   In this text there are clearly delineated sections to the text. It begins with an introduction, which is followed by a list of ingredients and then a method. It could also be argued that there is a conclusion to the text, although this is not separately paragraphed.

◎   The recipe is much more precise than Elinor Fettiplace's, although there are some points at which the reader is given some choice over ingredients and method.

◎   This 'choice', though, is not an open choice – Gary Rhodes clearly favours one over the other. This preference can be seen by the way Gary Rhodes 'himself' is a constant presence in the text. The narrator 'I' talks the narratee 'you' through the recipe, emphasising the various sensual experiences offered by this pudding.

◎   The bullet point above talks of a 'narrator', and there is a strong sense here of a story being told from beginning through to end. This is because Gary Rhodes, unlike Elinor Fettiplace, is writing for a mass audience. Because this book, with its high production costs such as colour photographs, is an offshoot of a celebrity cook television series, it could be argued that some readers will read the recipes but not make them. The recipe becomes, therefore, a form of entertainment as well as instruction.

◎   Obviously the vocabulary here will present few problems in understanding, but the text has something of a conversational feel, echoing the way the recipe might be talked through on television. The use of 'pud' for pudding is part of this process.

Unit three (Text 14), p. 52

There are a number of ways to explore this data, which is rich in possible analysis and interpretations. In looking at topic management, therefore, only one possible line of enquiry is being followed.

101

One way of analysing data like this is to produce a sort of 'map' of how topics are discussed. It is possible to see that there are three topics here, although sometimes they can be seen to overlap. Greetings sequences, which are usually seen as phatic, are included here as a 'topic'. The three topics therefore are:

1   greetings;

2   concerns about the contact with Swedish students and knowledge of other languages;

3   concerns about a psychology essay that is due in.

It is then possible to trace a topic through the chat by using a different type style for each topic. (Note: one of the features of the software is that if a participant presses 'enter' twice, they are cloned, and their message does not always load up properly. This accounts for Rosie Wayman becoming Rosie Wayman_ #2 and possibly also for the lines 'omeuril/cpt lcomputer ill' later in the data.)

This process can be seen in the following section, where topic 1 is underlined, topic 2 is in *italics* and topic 3 is in **bold**.

Becca Wood>>**have you started your psychology essay yet (changing the subject a little)**
->->->->Andrew Turner connected at: Tue Feb 22 2000 10:56:59
Rosie Wayman>> *the hole language barrier scares me and what if I have nothing to say*
Becca Wood>>*I know what you mean, i can say I love you in swedish, but I don' think that will be very useful*
->->->->Andrew Turner disconnected at: Tue Feb 22 2000 10:57:39
Rosie Wayman_#2>>**no I haven't started my essay, i have loads of books but i need another one before I start**
Becca Wood>>**same here**
Rosie Wayman_#2>>*i love you i can't say anything*
Becca Wood>>*actually it might be norwegen, which i can say i love you in*
Rosie Wayman_#2>>**do you understand the essay questions**
Becca Wood>>i tend to talk rubish, i'm sorry, i've got wafflyitus
->->->->Jennifer Kirk connected at: Tue Feb 22 2000 10:59:12
Becca Wood>>**i understand it ish, but i still have no idea what to write**
Jennifer Kirk>><u>hel 1 1 1 1 1 1 1 1 1 loooooooooooo</u>
Becca Wood>><u>hi there</u>
Rosie Wayman_#2>>*as a child I was taught french welsh and german and now I have a right mix so I have given up*

```
Becca Wood>>how's it goin Jen
Jennifer Kirk>>not tooooooo bad
Rosie Wayman_#2>>hi Jen
Jennifer Kirk>>hiya
Becca Wood>>can you speak fluently in those
Rosie Wayman_#2>>have you done the essay
```

What this shows is that the topic management here does not follow the patterns that we associate with the adjacency pairs of live talk – but that the participants are able to manage their chat without any apparent problems. So, Rosie and Becca cope without comment on the arrival and departure of the totally silent Andrew Turner, and then move from a two-way to a three-way conversation by integrating Jennifer into the chat.

Unit four, p. 56

The following are some points to consider:

◎ You will have drawn a small elephant – there is no possibility that you will have attempted a life size model!

◎ It is quite likely that you will have drawn the elephant in side profile. This is the most common way animals are represented in drawings, especially for children. If you are in a group, see if this is the most common response.

◎ Almost certainly you will have drawn the elephant's trunk – it would seem impossible to represent this animal without doing so.

◎ You may never in your life have seen an elephant – yet you know how to draw one.

◎ You may well have labelled the drawing with something to do with memory/forgetting, as this is a traditional representation of a quality supposedly possessed by elephants.

There may be other things you have noticed, and if you are in a group you can check what others have done, but the main point to make here is that, whatever your drawing skills, you will have easily understood the idea of *representing* something, and you will have assumed, quite rightly, that the child will understand aspects of representation too. In labelling the drawing you will have created a symbolic meaning, in that the human quality you give the elephant has no logical relationship with the creature.

Unit four, p. 57

There are many possible uses of this graphemic symbol. The following are a few examples:

- it can be a kiss on paper;

- it can be used as the mark for someone who cannot write;

- it can be ten in roman numerals;

- it can mark a vote in an election;

- it can mean a draw on the football pools;

- it can mark the centre of an area (X marks the spot);

- it can be a sign in algebra for an unspecified number;

- it can mean multiply in arithmetic;

- it can mean 'wrong' when your work is marked at school;

- it can mean cancelled if placed across an event poster;

- it can be used to mark 'deleted' letters, often in a taboo word, while still ensuring that the word is recognisable e.g. fxxk;

- it can replace the prefix 'ex' in such things as company names; if you look in your local telephone book you will find names such as 'XPress Ironing', 'Xpertise Training', 'Xtreme Talent Agency'.

Although no attempt is made here to date these uses, it will be clear that the last item in the list is likely to be recent, being part of the process whereby companies draw attention to themselves by using 'unusual' spellings of names. These only work, of course, when read silently. On the other hand the use of 'x' to mark your name is much less likely in an age when most people can write their name at least.

Other graphemic symbols include letters used to represent the quality of academic work, such as grades (with A always first or highest). There are many others which use the first letter of a word to represent its meaning such as 'P' for parking, 'F' for female etc. Again, though, it must be remembered that these graphemic symbols are culturally specific – they could mean something else in a different culture/language than ours.

Unit four (Text 18), p. 67

The text is designed to encourage people to use the Great Western Railway, by suggesting that they do not need to go abroad to have a good holiday. There are some interesting social class indicators here. Although at first it might seem to be an advertisement aimed at the rich, it is also aimed at the socially aspirant whose holiday in Cornwall, it is suggested, will be very like being in Italy.

One obvious way in which the visual and verbal combine is that they both directly address 'you', a constructed reader or narratee. Verbally the text has the word 'your', visually the two women look at the reader head on as though addressing 'you' to your face.

Visually, the text works in two halves, with Cornwall being presented as similar to Italy. Various semiotic system are at work here. The map of Cornwall is made to look like the map of Italy, even down to the very 'modern' detail of both maps breaking out of their boxes. The two women, who are drawn figures, have some difference in costume, but are facially similar. They are standing on a shared piece of land that is Cornwall to the west and Italy to the east. Behind them are fruits – presumably oranges in Italy and apples in Cornwall. These fruits can be seen as symbols of fertility.

Verbally there is writing at the top and bottom of the text, this time spanning across the two sections. A different job is done in each place. At the top of the text, and so given primary place, is the company name. Beneath this is a sales tag in the form of an imperative – but the idea of doing something 'first' only makes sense when it is read alongside the visual material underneath.

The rest of the written text is taken up with finding similarity between the two places, although because readers are being urged to travel to Cornwall, there is a strong sense that we would really like to go to Italy and need to be persuaded that Cornwall is just as good. The 'slogan' sounds rather awkward and unmemorable to modern ears – 'great similarity' does not carry the selling force we would expect nowadays. 'Both' technically refers to two, but here there are three qualities that are mentioned. Presumably two of these, 'shape' and 'beauties' could be seen as referring to the two women, so although the advertisement is hardly selling sex in the way modern holiday advertisements do, there is a strong hint of semantic play here.

Unit five, p. 79

1   Hopefully according to prescriptive grammar can only be used as an adverb meaning 'with hope' – so 'correct' usage would be 'I hope the bus will come soon'.

2   'Us', according to prescriptive grammar, should be replaced by 'we', even though it sounds strange.

3   Some idioms are subject to change, once their original source is lost. This idiom was originally 'off his own bat', a sporting reference. Another idiom which is apparently shifting in meaning, rather than in terminology, is 'it will all come out in the wash' which used to mean something like 'it will all be sorted in the end' but now means 'will be made public, exposed'.

4   This is a spelling issue – although many English words begin with 'al', traditionally and prescriptively, 'all right' has been two separate words.

5   'Disinterested' used to mean 'unbiased', so strictly speaking the word should be 'uninterested'.

6   The infinitive, which strictly speaking is required here, is 'try to', not 'try and'.

Unit six, p. 91

This text, which is designed to attract successful, go-ahead people uses a number of 'new' words as part of its strategy. Perhaps the most obvious are the initialisms such as 'OTE', 'BoSIS', 'BCM' and 'PCM', although most of these are explained in the text. It is expected that commercial initialisms and acronyms, such as 'HBOS' and 'BUPA' will be known already, though. The abbreviation 'k' replaces the numbers for a thousand.

There are also some blends: 'uk-wide', 'top-end', 'open-ended' are all connected by hyphens, and business/corporate by what is now known as a slash.

There are many noun phrases: 'market leading position in long-term savings and investment' is just one example of many.

Unit six, p. 92

It is likely that most responses to this task will have immediately focused on what is 'wrong' in terms of present day standard spelling. In fact, though, more words in both texts are the same as modern standard spelling than are different. Some patterns can be seen in the Shakespeare text, and it is usually helpful when discussing spelling to look for patterns. The most common feature is what would be seen now as extra letter 'e': 'worlde', 'mee', 'selfe' etc. Some double letters have now been lost as in 'proppe' and 'hopefull'. The word 'unpolisht' suggests that 'ed' at the end of a past tense had not yet been regularised.

The spelling in the email is again largely 'correct' but where there are changes from standard they can be accounted for in two broad ways. The first is speed of typing and a feeling that it is not necessary to proofread the text as in 'certianly'. The second, and most obvious feature are the devices to increase speed (and perhaps establish a certain narrative voice): so many apostrophes are omitted, and some words are shortened while still remaining recognisable as in 'shd', 'cld','wld'.

Unit six, p. 93

The recipe predominantly has two pieces of punctuation, the comma and the ampersand (&), often together. Instead of setting out various lists of ingredients and instructions, an ampersand is used at the point where a new item is introduced. The ampersand was originally used by medieval scribes as an abbreviation, but here it is used more as a marker to signify a break.

The email has no commas, which helps to give its created voice a breathless urgency. This also helped by occasional dashes, to suggest a slight change of topic. Most noticeable, though, is the use of multiple exclamation marks to stress an emotional response.

Unit six, p. 95

Much of the football text is metaphorical in origin, but because the language has become so associated with football, this may not necessarily be obvious. Just a few examples are 'open goal', 'missed penalties', 'hit', 'got closer' etc. The drama is also maintained by the use of metaphors: 'sank' and 'sunk' in the first paragraph, 'bawled his eyes out', 'hurl his arms round' and later 'sheer naked drama' are just a few.

When we look at Shakespeare we often tend to assume that his is the first use of metaphor, but this is not always the case. 'unpolisht lines', 'strong a proppe', 'idle houres', 'first heire of my invention prove deformed', 'barren a land/bad a harvest' are among the metaphors which sustain the flattery.

Both texts, then use metaphor to sustain their purpose, and most of the Shakespearean metaphor would still be understood today.

references

Bex, T. (1996) *Variety in Written English. Texts in society: societies in text*. London: Routledge.

Bowdman, M. (2004) *The Language of Websites*. London: Routledge.

Burchfield, R. (1981) *The Spoken Word, A BBC guide*. London: BBC.

Crystal, D. (2001) *Language and the Internet*. Cambridge: Cambridge University Press.

Goatly, A. (1997) *The Language of Metaphors*. London: Routledge.

Goddard, A. and Mean Patterson, L. (2000) *Language and Gender*. London: Routledge.

Goodman, S. and Graddol, D. (1996) *Redesigning English: new texts, new identities*. London: Routledge.

Harvey, K. and Shalom, C. (eds) (1997) *Language and Desire*. London: Routledge.

Hopper, R. (1992) *Telephone Conversation*. Bloomington, IN: Indiana University Press.

Lakoff, G. and Johnson, M. (1980) *Metaphors We Live By*. Chicago, IL: University of Chicago Press.

LINC (1992) *A Framework for Looking at Texts* in *Language in the National Curriculum: materials for professional development*. Nottingham: LINC, p. 84.

McArthur, T. (ed.) (1992) *The Oxford Companion to the English Language*. Oxford: Oxford University Press.

Mackinnon, D. (1996) 'Good and Bad English' in Graddol, D., Leith, D. and Swann, J. *English: history, diversity and change*. London: Routledge.

Pearsall, J. (ed.) (1998) *The New Oxford Dictionary of English*. Oxford: Clarendon Press.

Romaine, S. (1998) 'From Old English to new Englishes: unity in diversity', section 1.1 in *The Cambridge History of the English Language*, Volume IV. Cambridge: Cambridge University Press.

Shortis, T. (2001) *The Language of ICT*. London: Routledge.

Spurling, H. (ed.) (1986) *Elinor Fettiplace's Receipt Book*. London: Penguin.

index of terms

acronym 91
A word composed of the initial letters of the name of something, usually an organisation and normally pronounced as a whole word. For example, NATO (North Atlantic Treaty Organisation).

adjacency pair 46
These are pairs of spoken utterances that commonly occur, such as 'question/answer', 'introduction/greeting'.

affix 90
An addition to a word which changes its meaning. *See also* **prefix** and **suffix**.

attitudes and values 5
An attitude as used here is a way of thinking about something and a value is something that is believed in. When put together they refer to the ideology of a person or group.

back-formation 90
This involves making a new word by losing rather than adding an element to a word, so the verb 'to edit' comes from 'editor' and 'to commentate' from 'commentator'.

blending 91
Blending makes a new word by adding elements of two words together as in 'brunch', 'netiquette'.

borrowing 90
This involves taking a word from one language and using it in another language. Borrowings are also known as **loan words**.

chronology 26
This is to do with the way time is presented in a narrative.

clipping 91
This is a form of abbreviation, examples being 'veg', 'fan', 'deli'.

code-switching 87
The use by a speaker of more than one language or dialect in a conversation

collocation 49
This is the way certain words frequently appear together, often in a certain order e.g. 'fish and chips', 'salt and vinegar'.

compounding 91
This adds two words together as in 'body-blow', 'jet set', with such compounds sometimes using a hyphen to show that two words have been put together.

connotation 84
The connotations of a word are the associations it creates. These associations are often cultural.

creole 87
A pidgin language which becomes established in a community and so more widely used.

denotation 94
The literal dictionary definition of a word.

description *see* **prescription**.

dialogic 48
This refers to the ways in which different voices can be found within a text.

discourse structures 27
This refers to the rules and conventions which underlie the use of language in extended stretches of text.

dysphemism 73
A 'strong' term, often of disapproval – the opposite of euphemism.

ellipsis 17
Refers to the omission of part of a structure. It is normally used for reasons of economy and can create a sense of informality.

etymology 94
The study of the history of words including their origins and changes over time.

euphemism 73
A mild or evasive term for something that is taboo.

genre 5
An identifiable text type. It can be used in a number of ways: to identify a type of writing, such as in a report, a letter or a poem; and it can identify a group of texts which have subject matter in common, such as in sports writing, detective fiction.

gobbledygook 79
A critical term for language that is seen as deliberately opaque and full of jargon.

graphemic symbol 56
The smallest unit in written language – such as a letter of the alphabet.

graphology 5
This refers to the presentational features of texts, such as their shape, design or use of font.

ideology 6
A system of beliefs and ideas which is characteristic of a particular group or individual.

iconic 49
An iconic symbol visually suggests what it signifies.

idiom 40
A sequence of words which functions as a single unit of meaning and which cannot normally be interpreted literally. For example 'over the moon' means happy.

imperative 30
A command.

inflection 93
A change in the form of a word to express a grammatical function.

informalisation 39
This word is used by to describe the process whereby the language forms that were traditionally reserved for close personal relationships are now used in much wider social contexts such as education, business, politics etc.

initialism 17
Phrases that are referred to by their initial letters, e.g. BBC.

intertextuality 15
The way one text echoes or refers to another.

irregular verb 94
A verb that does not follow the general rules for verb forms, e.g. 'speak'.

lingua franca 87
A language adopted by speakers of different languages to allow communication to take place.

loan words *see* **borrowing**.

metaphor 28
The word 'metaphor' has a Greek origin meaning transference. It applies a description to something where it is not literally applicable. It is based on the idea of similarity between things which are nonetheless different.

modal verb 4
Modal verbs express notions of possibility, such as 'can' or 'could'.

multimodal 44
Forms of communication, such as emails, text messages and chat-rooms which use devices from a range of different communication systems at the same time.

narratee 4
The implied reader of a text, whose identity is built up by a series of assumptions that are made about the reader.

narrative 26
The way a story is told.

narrator 26
The voice telling the text, the person in a text who appears to be addressing the narratee.

neologism 22
A new word or an existing word with a new meaning.

noun phrase 4
A group of words which describe a noun.

parody 15
An imitation of a particular writer or genre.

pidgin 87
A contact language, often to allow trade, which has features of more than one language.

pragmatics 17
The factors that govern the choice of language in social interaction, and the effects these choices have.

prefix 90
An addition at the beginning of a word which changes its meaning e.g. 'un-fortunate'.

prescription (and **description**) 78
Prescriptive approaches to language lay down rules which should be followed, whereas descriptive approaches describe the language which is actually used.

relative clause 4
A clause which modifies a noun, often introduced by a relative pronoun such as 'who' or 'which'.

restricted language 87
A reduced and often specialised language devised with a particular purpose in mind, such as 'airspeak' spoken by pilots.

rhetorical 11
Rhetoric is the use of persuasive techniques.

semantics 5
Semantics is the study of meaning.

semiotics 55
Semiotics is the study of how we read **signs**. Within this two basic elements of meaning can be distinguished. The **signifier** is the actual marks on the page, the **signified** the meanings that can be found.

signified, signifier *see* **semiotics.**

signs *see* **semiotics.**

subordinate clause 4
A clause which normally cannot function on its own as a sentence.

suffixes 90
Additions at the end of a word which tend to change the class of a word and can at the same time expand upon its range of meaning. So the noun 'profession', which usually refers to certain types of occupation, gives the adjective 'professional' with its much wider range of meanings.

taboo 20
Language that is in some way 'forbidden'.

tautology 91
This means saying the same thing more than once.

eBooks – at www.eBookstore.tandf.co.uk

A library at your fingertips!

eBooks are electronic versions of printed books. You can store them on your PC/laptop or browse them online.

They have advantages for anyone needing rapid access to a wide variety of published, copyright information.

eBooks can help your research by enabling you to bookmark chapters, annotate text and use instant searches to find specific words or phrases. Several eBook files would fit on even a small laptop or PDA.

NEW: Save money by eSubscribing: cheap, online access to any eBook for as long as you need it.

Annual subscription packages

We now offer special low-cost bulk subscriptions to packages of eBooks in certain subject areas. These are available to libraries or to individuals.

For more information please contact webmaster.ebooks@tandf.co.uk

We're continually developing the eBook concept, so keep up to date by visiting the website.

www.eBookstore.tandf.co.uk